C000197863

Collins Gem

SPORTS RULES

Henry Russell

HarperCollins*Publishers*

The right of Henry Russell to be identified as the author of th
work has been asserted by him in accordance with the
Copyright, Designs and Patents Act 1988

HarperCollins*Publishers*
Westerhill Road, Bishopbriggs, Glasgow G64 2QT

First published 2002

Reprint 10 9 8 7 6 5 4 3 2 1 0

© Essential Books 2002

Conversions taken from *Collins Gem Measurements & Conversio*

ISBN 0 00 712271-3

Printed in Italy by Amadeus S.p.A.

Contents

Foreword

This book contains the rules for the world's most popular sports in a portable format. Sports rules are usually only found in large, heavy books or from the governing bodies of the various sports. The rules published by these governing bodies are often dauntingly detailed. For instance, the laws of cricket published by the Marylebone Cricket Club (or MCC) are about 17,000 words long. The rules of rugby run to more than 22,000 words.

All the entries here are up to date and feature the latest ratified changes. In addition to describing the rules, each entry lists the necessary equipment, describes the field of play (often with the aid of a diagram) and features interesting facts about the game under discussion. So, if you do not know the sport in which the women's world record is currently greater than the men's, read on.

Different sports are measured by their governing bodies in different ways. Measurements are shown as metric unless the sport is most often referred to in imperial. This is kept consistent within each entry. Tables are provided as appendices to help individuals to convert measurements into the form which best suits them.

ATHLETICS

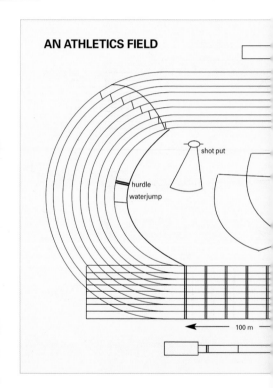

AN ATHLETICS FIELD

shot put

hurdle
waterjump

← 100 m

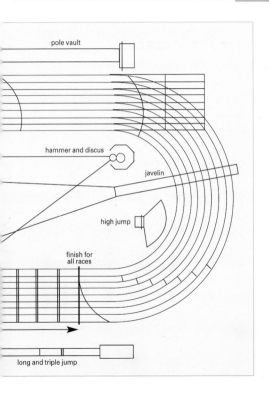

pole vault

hammer and discus

javelin

high jump

finish for
all races

long and triple jump

OLYMPIC ATHLETIC EVENTS – MEN

100 m	3,000 m steeplechase
200 m	20 km walk
400 m	50 km walk
800 m	High jump
1,500 m	Pole vault
5,000 m	Long jump
10,000 m	Triple jump
Marathon	Shot put
4 x 100 m relay	Discus
4 x 400 m relay	Hammer
110 m hurdles	Javelin
400 m hurdles	Decathlon

OLYMPIC ATHLETIC EVENTS – WOMEN

100 m	400 m hurdles
200 m	20 km walk
400 m	High jump
800 m	Long jump
1,500 m	Triple jump
5,000 m	Pole vault
10,000 m	Shot put
Marathon	Discus
4 x 100 m relay	Hammer
4 x 400 m relay	Javelin
100 m hurdles	Heptathlon

Introduction

Athletic (or 'track and field') contests are among the oldest of sports and were often held in conjunction with ancient religious festivals. For eleven centuries from 776 BC, the Olympic Games – then for men only – were enormously popular and prestigious events. The Romans continued the Olympic tradition until the time of the Christian emperor Theodosius, who banned the Games in AD 394. Athletics became popular again in the 19th century and the Olympics were revived in 1896.

Cross-country

Cross-country running usually takes place in autumn or winter when the ground is soft and the temperatures cool. Races may be run by individuals or teams of up to twelve in men's events and nine in women's and junior contests.

CLOTHING AND EQUIPMENT
- Shorts, shirt or vest with running numbers on front and back
- Running shoes, with or without spikes

FIELD OF PLAY

Races may vary greatly in length, but are typically between 3.2 and 19.3 km (2–12 miles) long. The recommended distances are: senior men 12 km (7.5 miles); junior men 8 km (5 miles); senior women 6 km (2½ miles); junior women 4 km (2½ miles).

> One-hour races are also popular. The world record distances covered in this time are currently 21.1 km (men) and 18.34 km (women).

Cross-countrys are run mainly over open country, heathlands and grassland; a limited amount of ploughed land is allowed. Roads should be used as little as possible. The first 1,500 m (1 mile) of any course should be unrestricted and, as far as possible, flat.

The course should be clearly marked with flags, which should be visible from at least 125 m (140 yd).

Road races may be of any length, up to and beyond 160 km (99.4 miles) (*see also* **Marathon**).

RULES

- Races begin with a pistol shot fired by the starter. A 5-minute warning may be given.
- At the end of a team race, the placings of the members are added together. The team with the lowest total is the winner.

Discus

Throwing the discus is one of the oldest of the track and field events. It has been popular since the ancient Greek Olympics.

CLOTHING AND EQUIPMENT

- Shirt, shorts, shoes
- Discus: plate-shaped rubber disc 219–221 mm in diameter; maximum central thickness 44–46 mm; minimum weight men 2 kg, women 1 kg

FIELD OF PLAY

The discus is thrown from a ring 2.5 m in diameter which broadens out into a landing area. This is a sector whose edges radiate at 40° from the centre of the circle.

RULES

- The aim is to throw the discus further than any opponent so that it lands within the marked sector.

- The thrower enters the ring and takes up position at the back. He rests the discus in the throwing hand then makes one-and-a-half quick turns before releasing it at shoulder level.

Hammer

Throwing the hammer has been a part of the Olympic Games since the time of the ancient Greeks.

CLOTHING AND EQUIPMENT

- Shirt, shorts, shoes, one glove
- Hammer: 117.5–121.5 cm long; minimum weight 7.26 kg
- Ball: diameter 110–130 mm
- Handle: a single or a double loop up to 10.5 cm long; no hinged joints; must not stretch during the throw

FIELD OF PLAY

The hammer is thrown from within a 2.135 m diameter circle into a marked target area. This is a sector whose edges radiate at 40° from the centre of the circle. For safety reasons, most of the throwing circle is surrounded by a metal cage, apart from the gap that gives access to the target area.

RULES

- The throw begins from a stationary position with the hammer head resting on the ground inside or outside the circle. The thrower then swings round, swirling the hammer until he is ready to release.

- The throw is a foul if, after commencing his action, the competitor touches with any part of his body either the top of the ring bounding the circle or the ground beyond it. It is also a foul throw if any part of the hammer lands outside the lines that mark the sector.

- Competitors must not leave the cage until their hammer has landed.

- Distances are recorded to the nearest 2 cm below the actual distance thrown.

- The winner is the competitor who makes the longest throw over six trials. In the event of a tie, the competitors' next-best throws are taken into consideration.

> Unusually, the women's Olympic record for discus is currently greater than the men's. Jürgen Schult threw 74.08 m in 1986, but this was surpassed two years later by Gabriele Reinsch, who threw 76.80 m.

High Jump

Over the past 50 years, high jumping styles have changed dramatically, from the 'scissors' technique, to the 'straddle', to the now-predominant 'Fosbury flop'.

In the scissors, the competitor keeps the body upright over the bar. In the straddle, the athlete approaches the bar and kicks the lead leg upward, then contours the body over the bar, face down.

The flop was popularised by Dick Fosbury, an American who developed the style and used it to win the 1968 Olympic gold medal. The athlete approaches the bar almost straight on, then twists his body on takeoff so that his back is facing the bar before landing in the pit. These landing areas, which at one time were recesses filled with sawdust, are now well-padded foam-rubber mats.

CLOTHING AND EQUIPMENT

- Shirt, shorts, shoes
- One crossbar: circular pole 4.02 m wide; maximum weight 2.25 kg
- Two uprights: rigid and extending at least 10 cm above the maximum height to which the crossbar can be raised

FIELD OF PLAY

The high jump is made over a crossbar which is raised after each round.

RULES

- Competitors remain in the contest until eliminated by three consecutive failures.

- After each round, the crossbar is raised by at least 2 cm.

- There is no limit to the length of the run-up that may be taken by high jumpers.

- The contestant must make the takeoff for the high jump using one foot only, not two.

Hurdles

Hurdle races are track events in which sprinters must not only run as fast as they can but also jump over a number of barriers in their way.

CLOTHING AND EQUIPMENT

- Shirt, shorts, running shoes
- Hurdles: metal with a wooden top bar; designed to be knocked down by forces of 3.6–4 kg

FIELD OF PLAY

Olympic hurdling events are held over distances of 110 m and 400 m for men and 100 m and 400 m for women.

Men hurdle over ten barriers 106.7 cm high in the 110 m, and ten barriers 91.4 cm high in the 400 m event. At some athletics meetings, particularly in the USA, equivalent distances of 109.7 m (120 yd) and 402.3 m (440 yd) are sometimes run.

In the women's 100 m, competitors must negotiate eight barriers, each 84 cm high.

RULES

- In races of this type, there is no penalty for knocking down hurdles, unless it is done deliberately with the hand. The rear leg or foot may not trail alongside the hurdle, but must be drawn over the top.

- All hurdle races are run in lanes; when the track is an oval, hurdles are always run in an anticlockwise direction.

Javelin

The javelin developed from the ancient martial art of
spear-throwing.

FIELD OF PLAY

A 36.5 m runway leads to the throwing mark. Beyond this
is a landing area over 100 m long in the shape of a sector
whose edges radiate at 40° from the throwing point.

CLOTHING AND EQUIPMENT

- Shirt, shorts
- Shoes with up to eleven spikes up to 12 mm long
  and 4 mm in diameter
- Javelin: spearlike shaft of wood or metal with metal
  tip and grip bound around the shaft at the
  approximate centre of gravity; length 260–270 cm
  for men, 220–230 cm for women; minimum weight
  800 g men, 600 g women

RULES

- The javelin is thrown from behind an arc and must land
  within the marked sector. Each thrower usually has three
  throws (trials), unless there are fewer than eight

competitors, in which case each competitor may throw six times.

- After a running approach along the runway, the competitor throws the javelin overhand. The javelin point must come down first for the throw to be legal. A throw is also judged a foul if the thrower touches the arc or any point beyond it.

- The throw is measured from the inner edge of the arc to the nearest mark made by the head of the javelin. Distances are recorded to the nearest 2 cm below the distance thrown.

- The winner is the competitor who throws his javelin the greatest distance. In the event of a tie, the winner is decided by the competitors' next-best throws.

Long Jump

Formerly known as the broad jump, the long jump has been contested since ancient times.

CLOTHING AND EQUIPMENT

- Shirt, shorts
- Spiked running shoes

FIELD OF PLAY

A 45 m cinder or synthetic runway with a wooden takeoff board at the end. The landing area is a sand-filled pit at least 9 m long and 2.75 m wide. It should be moistened before the competition begins and raked level after every jump.

RULES

- Contestants run at full speed along the runway to the takeoff board. At this point they must leave the ground. They may step on the board but must not allow any portion of the foot to go over it, otherwise it is a foul and the jump is invalid.

- Each legal jump is measured from the foremost edge of the takeoff board to the nearest break in the landing area made by any part of the competitor's body. Distances are recorded to the nearest centimetre below the distance jumped.

- Each competitor usually has three trials, unless there are fewer than eight contestants, in which case each has six attempts.

- In the event of a tie, the winner is the jumper whose next-best jump is longest.

Marathon

The marathon is a long-distance running race that commemorates the legendary run made by Pheidippides to bring news of the Greek victory over the Persians at the Battle of Marathon in 490 BC. Although these two places are 24 miles (38.6 km) apart, the modern event is now always run over 26 miles 385 yd (42.2 km), which was the distance raced at the 1908 London Olympics, where the gold medal was taken appropriately enough by another Greek, Spiridon Loues.

Today a world-class male runner can complete a marathon in just over 2 hours, but because of the vast differences in the courses, the International Amateur Athletic Federation does not recognise a world record.

CLOTHING AND EQUIPMENT

- Shorts
- Shirt or vest with running numbers on front and back
- Running shoes, with or without spikes

FIELD OF PLAY

Road running of marathon distance is increasingly popular, with races taking place over measured courses on city streets or country roads. Half marathons are also held regularly in many parts of the world.

The precise length of the modern Marathon is the distance between Windsor, Berkshire and the royal box at the old White City Stadium in London. These two points were the start and finish of the 1908 Olympic Marathon. The distance was standardised in 1924.

Pole Vault

Competitors use a flexible pole to vault a crossbar between two uprights. The crossbar is raised after each round and athletes remain in the competition until eliminated by three consecutive failures.

CLOTHING AND EQUIPMENT

- Shirt, shorts, shoes
- Pole: any length, any smooth, flexible material

FIELD OF PLAY

The runway should be 1.22 m wide and at least 40 m long. At the end of the runway, just beneath the bar, is a wedge-shaped depression known as a box, into which the competitor must thrust the leading end of his pole before jumping. The crossbar should be 4.3–4.37 m wide and the landing area should cover 5 m².

RULES

- After the completion of each round, the bar must be raised by a minimum of 5 cm. The exact height must be announced by the judges before jumping commences. Measurements are taken to the upper edge of the bar.

- A jump is a failure if the competitor touches the ground with any part of the pole or any part of his body, other than his feet, before clearing the bar; if he knocks the bar off its supports; or if he places his lower hand above the upper or moves the upper hand higher on the pole.

Relay

In relay races, teams of four athletes try to carry a baton from start to finish faster than any of their opponents.

CLOTHING AND EQUIPMENT

- Shirt, shorts, shoes (optional)
- Smooth, hollow batons; minimum weight 50 g

RULES

- Teams of four run separate legs, each of equal length. At the end of the first three legs, the runner passes on a baton to the next member of the team. This exchange may happen only in the take-over zones, specially marked-out stretches of the running track 20 m long.

- The runner who is due to receive the baton may start running from any point up to 10 m behind the rear end of the take-over zone, but he must receive the baton within the marked area. The last runner – sometimes known as the anchor – takes the baton to the finishing tape.

- There are four Olympic relay events: men's and women's 4 x 100 m and men's and women's 4 x 400 m. Some other athletics meetings feature 4 x 200 m relays.

- The 4 x 100 m races are run entirely in lanes; in other relays, the first two stages are run in lanes, as is the third until the runners leave the first bend, at which point they may break into any position they like. However, batons must be exchanged in the change-over zones assigned to each team at the start of the race.

Running Events

Running events may be held over many distances, but the races held at the Olympic Games are the 100 m, the 200 m, the 400 m, the 800 m, the 1,500 m, the 5,000 m and the 10,000 m.

CLOTHING AND EQUIPMENT

• Shirt, shorts, running shoes (optional)

FIELD OF PLAY

A running track divided into at least six lanes. In longer sprints on a curved track, the start is staggered so that runners in the outer lanes start further ahead of contestants inside them to their left, who have a smaller circumference to run around. All runners travel the same distance.

RULES

- Races up to 800 m are run entirely in lanes. In the 800 m, competitors may break into any position they like after the first bend. Over longer distances, they make break at any time as long as they do not obstruct any other runner.

- The winner is the runner whose torso first breaks the tape suspended directly above the finishing line.

- Races are timed either by mechanical watches or by electronic photo-timers that can measure finishes to hundredths of a second. Most running tracks have six or eight lanes. If there are more than these numbers of contestants, qualifying rounds (heats) are held to eliminate the slowest runners.

- Sprinters use a crouch-start in which, after the command 'On your marks' by the starter, the contestant kneels with one knee on the ground and both hands resting behind the starting line. On the 'Get set' command, the sprinter raises the knee from the ground in anticipation of the gun. When the gun fires, the runner will break as quickly as possible from the starting line.

- To facilitate a quick getaway, starting blocks are used to give the runner something to push off against.

Shot Put

In the shot put, athletes throw a heavy ball from a circular base constructed of concrete or synthetic material. Each competitor usually has three throws, unless there are fewer than eight entrants, in which case each has six attempts. The winner is the contestant with the longest throw. A tie is decided by the competitors' next-best throws.

CLOTHING AND EQUIPMENT

- Shirt, shorts, shoes
- Shot: metal ball weighing 7.2 kg for men, 4 kg for women

FIELD OF PLAY

The shot circle is 2.1 m in diameter and has a toeboard at the front of it.

RULES

- In the 'O'Brien' technique, the most popular style, the athlete is positioned at the back of the ring, with the shot tucked under the chin. The contestant crouches low on one foot with his or her back to the toeboard, then thrusts to the front of the ring, there throwing the shot forwards.

- The athlete may touch the near side of the toeboard but must not touch the top of it.

- Distances are measured from the inner edge of the toeboard to the nearest mark made by the shot. They are recorded to the nearest 1 cm below the distance put.

Steeplechase

The Olympic steeplechase is a men's event run over 3,000 m. It comprises 28 hurdle jumps and seven water jumps.

CLOTHING AND EQUIPMENT

- Shirt; shorts; running shoes
- Six hurdles: wooden barriers weighing 80–100 kg, 91.4 cm high with crossbars 12.7 cm wide

FIELD OF PLAY

An oval running track with six or more lanes. The hurdles are positioned across the three inside lanes only. The third and fourth hurdles are put in position after the hurdlers have passed by on the first lap. Hurdlers run outside the water jump on the first lap.

RULES

• Runners jump all obstacles at least four times. The winner completes the distance in the shortest time.

Triple Jump

In the triple jump, contestants hop, step and jump from a runway into a landing area.

CLOTHING AND EQUIPMENT

• Shirt; shorts; running shoes

FIELD OF PLAY

The runway is a cinder or synthetic track 45 m long and 1.22 m wide.

The wooden takeoff board is situated 13 m before the end of this runway.

The landing area is beyond the front edge of the runway. It is a sand-filled pit at least 9 m long and 2.75 m wide.

RULES

When the athlete reaches the board, he takes off and lands on the same foot; then, while attempting to maintain momentum, he takes an exaggerated step, landing on the opposite foot and continues into the pit with a third jump, landing on both feet.

> The current world record holder in the men's triple jump is Britain's Jonathan Edwards with 18.29 m (59 ft 5 in). The women's holder is Inessa Kravets (15.5 m/50 ft 4 in). Both records have stood since 1995.

Each jump is measured from the foremost edge of the takeoff board to the nearest break in the landing area made by any part of the competitor's body. Distances are recorded to the nearest centimetre below the distance jumped.

The winner is the competitor who records the longest triple jump after six trials.

In the event of a tie, the winner will be the jumper whose second-best jump is longest.

GOVERNING BODY

British Athletic Federation
225A Bristol Road
Edgbaston
Birmingham B5 7UB

International Amateur Athletic Association
Website: http://www.iaaf.org

Atlanta 1996

GYMNASTICS

Introduction

OLYMPIC GYMNASTIC EVENTS – MEN

Floor exercises   Alloy rings
Horizontal bar   Vault
Parallel bars   Trampoline
Pommel

OLYMPIC GYMNASTIC EVENTS – WOMEN

Floor exercises   Rhythmic All-round
Beam   Rhythmic team
Asymmetric bars   Trampoline
Vault

The word gymnastics is derived from the ancient Greek
gymnazein, meaning 'to exercise naked'. Modern gymnasts
perform with their clothes on but they still adhere to the
original principle of combining physical strength with
acrobatic skills presented in an aesthetically pleasing manner.

In addition to the events described below, the modern
Olympics now features the trampoline and various
all-round rhythmic events for individuals and teams. While
the basic rules of these activities are so simple as to be

self-evident, the artistic criteria by which they are judged
are almost infinitely complicated (and to some degree
subjective).

Alloy Rings

The rings are a gymnastic exercise for men which tests
upper body strength and general physical flexibility.

CLOTHING AND EQUIPMENT
• Long leggings with stirrup straps, and vest

FIELD OF PLAY

The two alloy rings are suspended 50 cm apart at a height
of 275 cm above the ground. They hang from a frame
575 cm high and 280 cm wide.

RULES

• Exercises should display strength, swing and hold in
  roughly equal proportions. Specifically, each routine
  should contain at least one handstand executed from
  a swing, one handstand executed with strength, and
  two static held parts during which the rings should
  be stationary.

Asymmetric Bars

The asymmetric bars are used only in women's events.

CLOTHING AND EQUIPMENT

• Leotard

FIELD OF PLAY

Two wooden or fibreglass bars are placed 43 cm apart and parallel to each other but at different heights. The lower bar is 140–160 cm above the floor; the upper bar is 235–240 cm high.

RULES

• The compulsory exercises are as set out from time to time by the sport's governing body. In addition to various specific requirements, the most important features of any exercise are upward or circular swings, movements from swing to handstand, pirouettes (turns around the longitudinal axis of the body), saltos (turns around the short axis of the body), and flight elements.

• There must be at least ten elements in every exercise.

- Only four elements may be performed consecutively on the same bar; the gymnast must then change bar, touch the other bar, or dismount.

- The exercise should be harmonious and contain no stops or interruptions.

The asymmetric bars was one of three events in which Nadia Comaneci of Romania won the gold medal at the 1976 Olympic Games in Montreal. She scored 10 in her initial exercise, the first perfect score in Olympic competition. She was 14 years old at the time and weighed only 39 kg.

Beam

The balance beam is a women's event that has become a popular Olympic sport.

CLOTHING AND EQUIPMENT

- Leotard

FIELD OF PLAY

The beam is covered in suede and measures 5 m x 10 cm. The top edge of the beam should be 120 cm above the mat.

RULES

- Each competitor is required to perform a balanced routine of movements lasting 70–90 seconds and making use of the whole length of the beam.

- The routine is timed from the moment the gymnast's feet leave the floor until she returns to it. If she falls, she must resume within 10 seconds or be disqualified.

Women gymnasts peak early. The beam was one of three gold medals won by 17-year-old Olga Korbut of the Soviet Union at the 1972 Munich Olympics.

- Each routine should contain a mixture of compulsory and optional elements. The compulsory requirements may be varied from time to time by the sport's governing body. All routines should include acrobatic elements with a flight phase, strength elements, gymnastic elements (turns, leaps, steps, runs), balance elements (adopting sitting, standing or lying positions), and dance steps.

- Points are deducted by the judges for monotony of presentation and/or movement; omission of any of the required elements; supporting a leg against the side of the beam; falling off; or more than three pauses.

Floor Exercises

Floor exercises are popular Olympic events performed by both sexes.

> ## CLOTHING AND EQUIPMENT
> - Leotard (women); shorts and vest (men)

FIELD OF PLAY

Floor exercises are performed on a mat which covers an area measuring 12 m².

RULES

- Each men's exercise should last 50–70 seconds; women's floor exercises are 70–90 seconds long.

- Exercises contain both compulsory elements, as laid out from time to time by the sport's governing body, and various optional elements.

- Men's exercises must include three different acrobatic connections (smooth and artistic transitions from one phase of the exercise to the next), one strength element and a static element of balance on one arm or leg.

- Points may be deducted for taking more than three steps, stepping out of the area, or for too long or too short a performance.

- Each women's routine must incorporate acrobatic elements, acrobatic strength elements, gymnastic elements (turns, leaps, steps, runs, arm swings), balance elements in sitting, standing or lying positions, and dance steps.

> Women's exercises are accompanied by music; men's events are performed in silence.

- Points may be deducted by women's judges for monotony, lack of high points, exaggerated theatricality or stepping out of the area.

- In both men's and women's events, full use should be made of all available floor space.

Horizontal Bar

The horizontal bar is a men's event.

CLOTHING AND EQUIPMENT

- Shorts and vest

FIELD OF PLAY

The bar is made of high tensile steel. It is 240 cm long and stands 275 cm above the mat.

RULES

• Each exercise contains both compulsory and optional elements, all of which should be performed with swinging movements and without pause or interruption.

• The elements that must be included are giant forward and backward swings; movements close to the bar; turns around the long axis of the body; and flights that begin and end with both hands on the bar. All exercises must conclude with a proper dismount, typically a double somersault and a two-footed landing.

Parallel Bars

The parallel bars are an apparatus used in men's gymnastic events. The emphasis is on upper-body strength and general physical flexibility.

CLOTHING AND EQUIPMENT

• Shorts and vest

FIELD OF PLAY

The exercises are performed on two laminated wooden bars 350 cm long placed parallel to each other 42 cm apart and at the same height of 195 cm above the mat.

RULES

- Exercises should be harmonious and contain no stops or interruptions. Routines typically include extended forward and backward giant swings through 360°, combined with changes of direction and grip, as well as release and re-grasp movements. The high dismounts from the bar allow the gymnast to show his acrobatic talents and landing prowess.

> Every routine should feature at least ten different movements both above and below the bars.

- The compulsory elements are as set out from time to time by the sport's governing body.

Pommel

This event is for men only and involves compulsory and optional elements. All three parts of the pommel horse – the surface and both handrails – must be used.

CLOTHING AND EQUIPMENT

- Long leggings with stirrup straps, and vest

FIELD OF PLAY

The pommel horse stands 115 cm high and is 160 cm
across. In the middle of its upper side are two handrails.

RULES

- Each exercise must comprise different types of circular
  and pendulum swings in various positions of support on
  all parts of the horse, at least two scissor-type
  connections, and an element performed on one
  handle only.

- Double leg circles must predominate.

Vaulting

After a short run-up, each vault lasts no longer than a couple of seconds, but the best gymnasts manage to cram complicated, often breathtaking moves into that moment.

CLOTHING AND EQUIPMENT

- Leotard (women); shorts and vest (men)

FIELD OF PLAY

The horse for the men's vault is 135 cm high; for women it is 120 cm high.

The springboard is placed in line with the long axis of the horse in the men's event and in line with the short axis for the women's.

RULES

- Each gymnast performs one compulsory vault, then two optional vaults, neither of which may be the same as the compulsory. For the optional vaults, the better mark awarded is the one that counts.
- All vaults are graded A–D, depending on their degree of difficulty, and divided into eight types. Gymnasts must indicate in advance which vault they are about to attempt.

- The vault is divided into four phases: the first flight phase; the support/strike phase; the second flight phase; and the landing. The run-up is not evaluated, although points are deducted if it exceeds the maximum permitted distance of 25 m.

Compulsory vaults change from time to time. From 1981 to 1984, for example, women's events demanded a stretched first flight, then a handspring, followed by a full turn about the longitudinal axis during the second flight.

- All vaults must be performed with the support of both hands on the horse.

- Male gymnasts are required to begin their flight 2 m from the horse and gain a height of 1 m above it.

- Each judge scores the vault by making deductions from a maximum possible of 10 points.

GOVERNING BODY

Fédération Internationale de Gymnastique
Rue des Oeuches 10
Case postale 359
2740 Moutier
Switzerland

Website: http://www.fig-gymnastics.com

American Football

American football came to
prominence in the 19th century.
It is thought to have evolved
from the English games
Rugby and **Football**.

The game is played by two teams of eleven
players who attempt to score points by field goals kicked
through the upright goalposts or by putting the ball behind
their opponents' goal line in an approved manner. Teams
advance the ball by running with it, passing (throwing) it,
and kicking it towards the opponents' goal line.

There are three sets of rules: one for professionals, one for
colleges, and one for high schools.

CLOTHING AND EQUIPMENT

- Protective helmet, shoulderpads, kneepads and
  gloves
- Stockings and shoes with steel cleats
- Specially padded trousers, jerseys, wristbands
- Ball: inflated rubber in a leather case; oval
  (length 11–11¼ in; circumference 21¼–21½ in;
  weight 14–15 oz)

FIELD OF PLAY

The field is known as a gridiron because of the way it is marked out, with latitudinal stripes every 5 yd. The playing area is 53⅓ yd wide and 100 yd long with two additional 10 yd areas called end zones. The goal consists of two uprights and a crossbar.

RULES

- Teams are allowed to make unlimited substitutions, but may have no more than 40 players in uniform.

- A touchdown is scored when a player carries the ball over the opponents' goal line or passes the ball to a team-mate, who either catches the ball in the end zone or catches it within the playing area and carries it over the goal line. A touchdown scores 6 points.

- Teams may also score by kicking the ball between the uprights above the crossbar of the end zone that the opponent is defending. This is known as a field goal and counts 3 points.

- Points can also be scored by stopping an opponent with the ball behind that opponent's own goal line (a safety, worth 2 points) and on a conversion play following a touchdown.

- In a conversion attempt, the team that has scored the touchdown may either attempt to kick the ball through

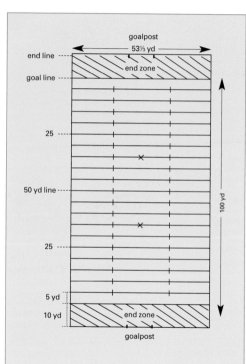

goalpost

53⅓ yd

end line

end zone

goal line

25

50 yd line

25

5 yd

10 yd

end zone

goalpost

100 yd

the uprights or advance it across the goal line again from the opponents' 2 yd line (3 yd line in college football).

> In 1860 American football was banned at Harvard University because the professors thought it was too dangerous.

- In the US National Football League (NFL), both types of conversion plays are worth 1 point; in college games, kicking is worth 1 point, but advancing over the goal line by a run or a pass is worth 2 points.

- College and professional games are 60 minutes long; high school games last 48 minutes. Play is divided into two halves, and the halves are divided equally so that in a complete game there are four quarters. But games actually last much longer, because the clock is stopped after scores and for penalties, measurements, injuries, incomplete passes, and when the ball goes out of bounds. Teams are allowed to take three 1½ minute time-outs per half to make substitutions and plan tactics; they also leave the field at half-time.

- The captains toss a coin to decide who will start the game. Play begins with a kickoff, in which a member of one team place kicks or drop kicks the ball from his own 35 yd line in NFL games or from the 40 yd line in college and high-school play.

- Subsequent plays are begun with the centre hiking the ball (passing it backward through his legs) to a quarterback stationed directly behind him from the point (called the scrimmage line) to which the centre's team has advanced the ball. A play ends when the ball-carrier – either a rusher (runner) or a pass-receiver – is tackled by an opponent, falls to the ground (in professional football, he must be tackled to the ground) or runs out-of-bounds, or when a forward pass is not completed (caught by a team-mate).

- The offensive team (the team in possession of the ball) lines up in different formations, dictated by strategy, and is allowed four plays, known as downs, to advance the ball 10 yd.

- Each time a team advances the ball 10 yd, it is credited with a first down and is given four more downs to make the advance again. If the team fails to advance 10 yd in any series of four plays, the opposition takes possession of the ball. Often a team that is stopped deep in its own territory with little chance of making the 10 yd will kick the ball in order to drive the opposition back into their own territory.

- At any point in the game, the defence can get the ball by intercepting a pass or recovering a fumble (dropped ball). Generally, football teams have specialists for both offence and defence, and the same players do not participate in both phases of the game, although they are allowed to.

- When the ball goes out of bounds, play is re-started with a scrimmage. Here each team provides a line of at least seven players who stand on either side of the ball parallel to the goal line. The ball is fed into the neutral zone between them, and players then try to gain possession of it and feed it backwards with a snap – a pass through the legs – to the other members of their team, who must be at least 1 yd behind the scrimmage line.

- When a player on one team kicks the ball into the air, an opposing player may claim the right to catch the ball by raising one hand at full stretch above his head and waving it from side to side. He is then entitled to field the ball without being tackled or impeded. If he catches it, the ball becomes dead at that spot and the captain of his team must choose whether to put the ball back into play with a snap or a free kick.

- If an American football game is tied, there is a 15-minute period of sudden death; the first team to score is the winner.

GOVERNING BODY

National Football League (NFL)
280 Park Ave
New York, NY 10017
USA

Website: http://www.nfl.com

Archery

Archery – the art of shooting an arrow from a longbow –
has been practised by hunters for at least 30,000 years. The
bow and arrow were the principal weapons of warfare
until their role was taken over by gunpowder. Today target
archery is a popular competitive sport. The *Fédération
Internationale de Tir à l'Arc* (FITA) has held world
championships since 1931.

CLOTHING AND EQUIPMENT

- Close-fitting clothes that do not catch in bowstring
- Bow: length 1.8 m men, 1.7 m women
- Arrows: length 61–81 cm; weight usually under 28 g
- Targets: circular and made of straw ropes stitched
  together; two standard diameters: 122 cm and
  80 cm; bottom of target stands 61 cm above ground

FIELD OF PLAY

In a FITA round, an archer must shoot 12 rounds (36
arrows) each at distances of 90 m, 70 m, 50 m and 30 m.

The target is divided into ten concentric bands of different
colours and equal width: 6.1 cm on the larger target and
4 cm on the smaller. From the centre out, the scoring is as

follows: gold inner bull's-eye, 10; gold outer, 9;
red inner, 8; red outer, 7; blue inner, 6; blue outer, 5; black
inner, 4; black outer, 3; white inner, 2; white outer, 1.

RULES

- Each archer normally fires three arrows in a round.
  Scores are updated after every six arrows at longer
  distances and three at shorter distances.

- An arrow touching two colours or a dividing line scores
  the higher value. An arrow rebounding from or passing
  through the target will count only if its mark is
  identifiable. An arrow embedded in another arrow
  scores the same as that arrow.

- In the event of a tie, the winner is the archer who has
  scored the greatest number of scoring hits. If it is still a
  tie, the winner is the archer with the most bull's-eyes,
  then the most 9s, then the most 8s. If a tie still persists,
  the archers are declared equal.

GOVERNING BODY

Fédération Internationale de Tir à l'Arc (FITA)
Ave de Cour 135
CH1007 Lausanne
Switzerland

Website: http://www.archery.org

Badminton

Modern badminton is a game for two
or four players derived from the
ancient game of battledore and
shuttlecock. It is played mainly,
but not invariably, indoors.

CLOTHING AND EQUIPMENT

- Shirt, shorts or skirt, socks, rubber-soled shoes
- Racket: flat and identical on both faces with crossed
  strings; overall length 680 mm; head no more than
  290 mm long and 230 mm wide
- Shuttle: 25 mm in diameter at rounded base; no
  more than 68 mm at the top; weight 4.74–5.5 g
- The best shuttles have 16 goose feathers in a cork
  base; proprietary shuttles are plastic

FIELD OF PLAY

The court measures 13.4 m x 6.1 m. Across the middle is a
net 76 cm high, the bottom of which must be 1.55 m above
the ground.

RULES

- Service is decided by a toss. The winner can elect to serve or receive in the first game, or to choose to play at a particular end of the court. The loser of the toss makes the other choice.

- The server and receiver stand in the diagonally opposite service courts (always on the right at the start).

- Each service is delivered alternately from the right and left half of the court. The person serving must serve underhand and the receiver must stand still until the service is struck.

- A shuttle falling on a line is in.

- A point is won by hitting the shuttle on to the other side of the net so that it lands on the court before the opponent can return it.

- A point is lost if the shuttle is hit into or under the net, if it lands outside the opponent's court, if the shuttle touches a player or his clothing, or if a player hits the shuttle before it crosses the net.

- Matches are the best of three games. Each game starts at 0–0 ('love-all'). If the server wins a rally, he scores a point and serves again from the alternate service court. If the receiving side wins the rally, the score remains unchanged and the service passes to the next player in turn. In singles, this is the opponent; in doubles it is

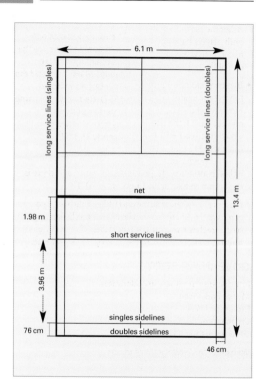

6.1 m

long service lines (singles)

long service lines (doubles)

13.4 m

net

1.98 m

short service lines

3.96 m

singles sidelines

76 cm

doubles sidelines

46 cm

either the partner or, if both players have just had a turn of serving, one of the opponents.

The major international team competitions are the Thomas Cup for men (inaugurated 1949) and the Uber Cup for women (1957). Badminton became a medal sport at the Olympic Games as recently as 1992.

- In men's badminton, 15 points win a game. However, if the score reaches 14–14, the side which first reached 14 can choose to play on to 15 or 17 points. In ladies' badminton, 11 points wins a game, and there is the option to play on to 13 points at 10–10.

- Players change ends at the end of both the first two games and again in the third game when the leading score reaches 8 in men's or 6 in ladies'. A 5-minute interval is allowed before the start of the third game.

GOVERNING BODY

International Badminton Federation

Manor Park Place
Rutherford Way
Cheltenham
Gloucestershire GL51 9TU

Website: http://www.intbadfed.org

Baseball

Baseball has its roots in the English game **Rounders** and became popular in North America, where it was codified in 1845 by Alexander Cartwright, Jr. The first professional baseball league was formed in 1871.

CLOTHING AND EQUIPMENT

- Team strip in uniform colours with numbers on the backs
- Helmets: must be worn by the catcher and all batters
- Gloves: worn on one hand by all defending players
- Ball: cork with yarn wound around it and a casing of stitched leather; weight 5–5¼ oz; diameter 2⅞ in
- Bats: generally wooden (in amateur games, aluminium is allowed); 3 ft 6 in long; up to 2¾ in thick

FIELD OF PLAY

The overall size of the fields on which baseball is played varies enormously – they are usually 250–450 ft from home base to the boundary – but the infield is always a square with 90 ft sides. The corner farthest from the outfield fence is the home plate, and the other bases – first, second, and third – run anticlockwise and are 60–65 ft apart. The outfield ends at a perimeter fence.

The pitcher's mound is an 18 ft circle sloping up towards a small, rectangular slab in the centre. The mound lies inside the square 60 ft 6 in from the home plate.

RULES

• Baseball teams (usually consisting of nine players) play nine innings, alternating in the field and at bat, with the home team always batting last. Each inning is divided into two halves known as the top and the bottom. The game is won by the side that scores most runs.

• The infielders – first baseman, second baseman, shortstop and third baseman – usually position themselves along the two sides of the square between first and second and second and third bases. The outfielders – left fielder, centre fielder, and right fielder – cover the respective portions of the outfield.

• The pitcher stands on the rubber mound and the catcher crouches behind the batter.

• The team at bat sends its nine men to the plate in a specified sequence. Each batter attempts to hit the pitcher's deliveries, which the latter tries to vary in speed and direction within the strike zone (the area over home plate and between the batter's knees and armpits).

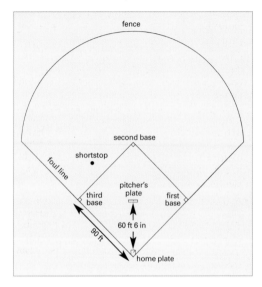

- A balk is an illegal pitch. It occurs if the pitcher's foot is not in contact with the plate when he delivers, if he pretends to pitch and does not do so, if he pitches when not facing the batter, if he drops the ball, or if he pitches when the catcher is not in position. A balk allows all base runners to advance to the next base.

- Substitutions are allowed throughout the game as long as the ball is dead. Players taken off may not come back on.

- Each team's half-inning consists of three outs. An out may occur in the following ways: when the pitcher gets three strikes on a batter; when a ball is caught before bouncing (a fly ball); when a ground ball is retrieved and thrown to first base before the batter arrives; when a base runner is not touching a base and is tagged (touched) by a fielder holding the ball; when a fielder who has the ball touches a base other than first when there is a runner approaching that base; when a player has left a base and is unable to get back before a caught fly ball is thrown to the base. Thus it is possible to get more than one out off a single pitch.

- A strike is any pitch at which the batter swings and misses, any pitch that travels through the strike zone, and any batted ball that lands outside the straight lines running from home plate through first base and from home plate through third base to the outfield fence (any such stroke is called a foul).

- The team at bat tries to get players on base and advance them until they round all four bases to score runs. The team with more runs after nine innings wins. If the score is tied at the end of nine innings, the teams play extra innings until one team scores more than the other and both teams have had an equal number of turns at bat.

- The most common way of reaching base is with a hit. However, a batter may also reach base if he is hit by a pitch, if he receives a walk by taking four pitches (called balls) outside the strike zone, if a defensive player misplays the ball for an error, if the catcher interferes with a swing, or if the catcher fails to catch the pitcher's throw on a third strike and does not throw the ball to first base before the batter reaches it.

> Although usually a nine-a-side game, since 1973 the American League and US colleges have allowed a tenth player, a designated hitter, to bat for the pitcher.

- Both the batter and runners may advance as far as possible on any hit. A one-base hit is a single, a two-base hit a double, a three-base hit a triple, and a four-base hit a home run. The most common kind of home run is a fair ball hit over the fence on a fly, but a batter may also run around all the bases before the fielders can retrieve a ball hit inside the park and throw it to the plate.

- Runners may also advance by stealing a base, on a balk (improper procedure by a pitcher), on a sacrifice bunt (a hit intended to move the runner even though the batter will be out), or on a sacrifice fly (a fly ball caught by an outfielder but not returned to the proper base before the runner reaches it, provided the runner does not leave his original base before the ball is caught).

• Four umpires, one near each base, regulate the game, enforce the rules, and call balls and strikes, foul and fair balls, and safe or out. The umpires may also eject players from the game for improper behaviour and call a forfeit for serious infractions. Some amateur games have only one or two umpires; the Championship Series between the American and National leagues, and the World Series have six.

GOVERNING BODY

International Baseball Federation
Ave de Mon Repos 24
Case Postale 131
1000 Lausanne 5
Switzerland

Website: http://www.baseball.ch

Basketball

Games similar to basketball have been played since prehistory. One early version, *pok-ta-pok*, was played by the Olmecs in Mexico in about 900 BC.

CLOTHING AND EQUIPMENT

- Each team's clothing must be of a different colour or colours from their opponents'; shirts have the player's number on chest and back
- Shorts, socks, basketball boots
- Ball: leather, rubber or synthetic material containing a rubber bladder; circumference 30–31 in; weight 1 lb 5 oz; should bounce 3 ft 11 in to 4 ft 6½ in when dropped onto a solid floor from 5 ft 10 in
- Two baskets: circular rings 1 ft 6 in in diameter; 10 ft above the ground in front of a backboard 5 ft 11 in wide and 3 ft 11 in high; hanging from each basket is an open-bottomed net

FIELD OF PLAY

Although basketball can be played outdoors, it was invented to serve as an exciting indoor exercise for the winter months in a northern climate.

The game is played on a court that must have a hard surface, not grass. There are no stipulated dimensions for the court, but it usually measures 91 ft 10 in plus or minus 13 ft in length and 49 ft 2 in plus or minus 6 ft 6 in wide. At each end of the court is a basket.

RULES

- Basketball involves two teams of five players each, plus up to seven substitutes. The object is to put a ball through a hoop, or basket, and thus score more points than the opposing team.

- Professional games are 48 minutes long, divided into four 12-minute quarters; college games, 40 minutes, played in halves; and high school games, 32 minutes, broken into quarters. If a game is tied at the end of regulation time, an overtime (3 to 5 minutes, depending on the level of competition) is played.

- At the start, the visitors choose ends; on neutral grounds, the captains toss a coin. Ends are changed after every quarter.

- The game starts with a jump ball where two players attempt to gain possession after a throw-up by the referee.

- Two points are given for a field goal, which is a shot that goes through the hoop while the ball is in play. Three points are awarded to a player who scores at a distance of 23 ft 11 in when facing the basket or 22 ft if he shoots from the sides, 'beyond the three-point line'. One point is awarded for a basket from a free throw, or foul shot, which is attempted by a player who has been fouled, or impeded physically by an opponent. Free throws are

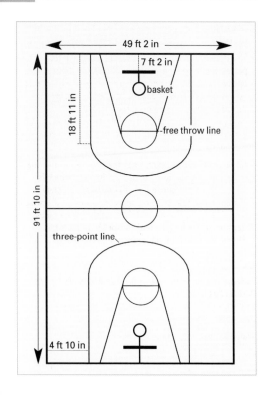

49 ft 2 in

7 ft 2 in

basket

18 ft 11 in

free throw line

91 ft 10 in

three-point line

4 ft 10 in

attempted, undefended, from a line drawn 15 ft from the basket.

- The defensive team can get the ball back by intercepting passes, blocking shots, or by stealing it out of an opponent's hand, provided that no illegal body contact occurs. After a basket is made, the ball is awarded to the other team, which puts it back in play. If a field-goal attempt is missed and the ball remains in bounds, it is kept in play by the team that recovers (rebounds) it.

- A player in possession may advance the ball by passing or rolling it to a team-mate or by dribbling, which is bouncing it along the floor with one hand. He may change hands only once during such a move, otherwise it is a foul known as double dribble. If the player takes steps while holding the ball without bouncing it as described above, it is a foul known as travelling.

GOVERNING BODY

Fédération Internationale de Basketball (FIBA)
PO Box 70 06 07
81306 Munich
Germany

Website: http://www.fiba.com

Billiards

Billiards developed in the 19th century. The World Professional Championships were first held in 1870, and there has been a World Amateur Championship since 1926. There are many different forms of billiards, but the most popular is the English version.

CLOTHING AND EQUIPMENT

- Professionals: black shoes, black trousers, a waistcoat and a bow tie, usually with a white shirt
- Three balls: one white, one spot white, and one red
- Cues: wooden, no less than 3 ft long

FIELD OF PLAY

English billiards is played on a baize-covered table 34 in high, measuring 12 ft x 6 ft, with a playing area of 11 ft 8½ in x 5 ft 10 in, the same as the table used for **Snooker**.

RULES

- One player's cue ball is the white; the other's is the spot white. Players use a cue to propel their cue ball towards the other two balls and score points either by pocketing balls (hazards) or by hitting both other balls (cannons).

- Each game (known as a frame) lasts either for an agreed length of time or until one player reaches an agreed number of points.

- Players lag or string (*see* **Snooker**) to determine who will break first and use which ball.

- The game begins with the red ball placed on the spot. The striker aims to hit it with his cue ball from the D. At the end of his turn, the other player brings his ball into play. He also makes his first shot from the D and may hit either of the balls on the table.

- Throughout the game, no shot may be made directly at any ball in the baulk area. A cushion must be struck first.

- If at any time the striker's ball comes to rest against another ball, the red is replaced on its spot. The non-striker's ball, if on the table, is placed on the centre spot; if it is off the table, it remains off and the striker plays from the D.

- If the non-striker's ball is pocketed during a break, it remains off the table until the break ends.

- Whenever the red is potted it is replaced immediately on the spot. When the cue ball is put down a hole, the striker brings it back into play by hitting it from the D.

- A cannon scores 2 points. Up to 75 consecutive cannons may be made in a single break. The striker also scores 2 points if the cue ball puts the other white into a pocket,

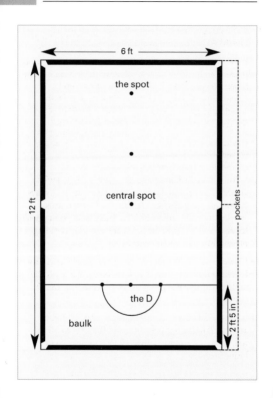

6 ft

the spot

central spot

12 ft

the D

baulk

pockets

2 ft 5 in

and 3 points if the cue ball hits the red into a pocket.

- If the cue ball goes into a pocket after a cannon, it scores an additional 2 points if the white ball was struck first, and 3 points if the red was struck first.

> When a good billiards player gets going, it is easy to imagine that his break will never end. In the 1934 world professional final, Walter Lindrum beat Joe Davis by the amazing score of 23,553 points to 22,678.

- It is a foul stroke if the player plays with both feet off the floor, plays a stroke before all the balls are stationary, strikes the ball with anything other than the cue, plays the wrong ball, plays out of turn, or plays from outside the D when he is supposed to play from within it. There is no point penalty for any of these fouls: the turn ends and the offending player loses his score for that turn.

- However, a player concedes points to his opponent for touching the ball twice (1 point), forcing a ball off the table (3 points), not playing out of baulk from the D (1 point), and push shots (1 point).

- If the cue ball goes 'in off' the other white, 2 points are added to the opponent's score. If it goes in off the red, there is a 3-point penalty. These are known as losing hazards.

GOVERNING BODY

World Professional Billiards and Snooker Association (WPBSA)

27 Oakfield Road
Clifton
Bristol BS8 2AT

Bowls

Prehistoric in origin, bowls was played in various forms by the ancient Egyptians, Greeks and Romans. It was popular in England by the 12th century.

CLOTHING AND EQUIPMENT

- Shoes with smooth rubber soles and no heels
- Woods: balls 12.1–13 cm in diameter; weight 1.42–1.59 kg; four per player. Each wood must have a bias, an approved degree to which it deviates from a straight line as it travels across the green.
- Jack: white ball 6.35 cm in diameter; weight 283 g

FIELD OF PLAY

A bowling green is a square with 36.57 m sides divided into six parallel rinks or lanes, each measuring 5.5–5.8 m

across (outdoors) and 4.6–5.8 m across (indoors). White wooden pegs with green thread drawn tightly between them mark the boundary of each rink. Several different games may take place on a green simultaneously.

Outdoor bowling greens are surrounded by a ditch 20–38 cm wide and 5–20 cm deep. Beyond the ditch is a bank which should be no less than 23 cm above the level of the green.

RULES

- Bowls is played outdoors or indoors on a grass or artificial surface. Games may be singles contests between two players, or between two teams of up to four. Each player normally rolls four woods in each round (called an end).

- The first player rolls the jack along the rink. It must come to rest at least 21 m from the front edge of the mat and at least 2 m before the ditch. The other players then try to get their woods as close to the jack as possible. When they bowl, players must keep one foot on or directly above a mat at the edge of the rink.

CROWN GREEN BOWLS

In one popular variation the green is 25–50 m square with a raised 'crown' about 15–30 cm higher than the edge at its centre.

- If the jack is driven into the ditch, the end is dead and must be re-started.

- At the completion of an end, each bowl closer to the jack than an opponent's scores 1 point. The game is over either after a specified number of ends (usually 21 for four-person teams) or at a specified game point (21 in singles).

- While attempting to get their woods as close as possible to the jack, players may also try to knock their opponents' balls out of the way into worse positions.

GOVERNING BODY

English Bowling Association
Lyndhurst Road
Worthing
West Sussex BN11 2AZ

Website: http://www.bowlsengland.com

Boxing

The so-called manly art of
self-defence – two men
hitting each other with their
fists – dates back thousands of years.
It entered the Olympic Games in about 688 BC
and was codified in its present form in 1866 by the
English Marquess of Queensberry.

CLOTHING AND EQUIPMENT

- Shorts, light boots or shoes, socks
- Amateurs wear red or blue vests (the colour
  depends on which corner they are in); professionals
  fight with bare torsos
- No rings or jewellery
- Gloves: leather, no finger-holes except for the
  thumb; weight from 227 g (8 oz) (amateur bouts), or
  170 g (6 oz) (professional and all title bouts).

FIELD OF PLAY

The boxing ring is actually a square 3.7–6.1 m (12–20 ft)
on each side and enclosed on all four sides by three or
four ropes.

RULES

- Modern boxing matches fought under Queensberry Rules are divided into a specified number of rounds, each usually 3 minutes long, with 1-minute rest periods between rounds.

> Queensberry Rules were intended to make boxing less gory. Gouging, wrestling and hitting below the belt were outlawed and gloves became mandatory.

- Amateur fights consist of 3 rounds, professional fights of 4 to 15 rounds. Championship fights are 12 rounds long.

- The sport has several different governing bodies, each keen to achieve top billing for itself, and as a result detailed regulations may vary. In all boxing, however, winners are determined by a decision of either the judges (who keep points or round victors on a scorecard as the fight progresses), the referee, or both.

- The winner may be decided by a knockout, in which one rival is sent to the floor by a punch and cannot get up within 10 seconds. A doctor or referee can declare the boxer injured or defenceless and stop the fight even if there is no knockdown. A tied or even match is ruled a draw.

- All boxers must weigh in on the day of the fight to make sure that they are fit and within the bounds of their weight category.

BOXING WEIGHT DIVISIONS

Category	Maximum Weight	
	Amateur	**Professional**
Light flyweight	48 kg (106 lb)	49 kg (108 lb)
Flyweight	51 kg (112 lb)	51 kg (112 lb)
Bantamweight	54 kg (119 lb)	53.5 kg (118 lb)
Featherweight	57 kg (126 lb)	57 kg (126 lb)
Junior Lightweight	——	59 kg (130 lb)
Lightweight	60 kg (132 lb)	61 kg (134 lb)
Light welterweight	63.5 kg (140 lb)	63.5 kg (140 lb)
Welterweight	67 kg (148 lb)	66.6 kg (147 lb)
Light middleweight	71 kg (156.5 lb)	70 kg (154 lb)
Middleweight	75 kg (165 lb)	72.5 kg (160 lb)
Light heavyweight	81 kg (179 lb)	79 kg (175 lb)
Cruiserweight	——	88.5 kg (195 lb)
Heavyweight	91 kg (201 lb)	over 88.5 kg (195 lb)
Superheavyweight	over 91 kg (201 lb)	——

GOVERNING BODY

British Boxing Board of Control
Jack Petersen House
52a Borough High St
London SE1 1XW

Website: http://www.bbbofc.com

Canoeing and Kayaking

Canoeing and the related sport of kayaking have been pastimes for many centuries. Their roots go back to the North American Indian canoe and the Eskimo kayak. The origins of the competitive and organised sport, however, can be more formally traced to the foundation in 1866 of the Royal Canoe Club in England. The sport was introduced to the Olympics at Berlin in 1936.

CLOTHING AND EQUIPMENT

- Canoe or kayak
- Competitors wear black numbers with a white background on their backs
- Paddles: spoon-shaped; usually made of fibreglass or wood; kayak paddles have two blades, Canadian canoe paddles have only one

---

FIELD OF PLAY

Three basic events are held: slalom, in which racers travel a course of rough rivers with steep falls and treacherous turns around gates; wild water, in which they race straight forward through rough waters; and sprint or distance, in which the course is over still water.

RULES

• Although the terms canoe and kayak are often used interchangeably, there are important differences between the two types of vessel. A canoeist kneels and uses a single-blade paddle, whereas a kayakist sits and uses a double-blade paddle. A canoe is open at the top; a kayak is enclosed. Kayaks may have steering rudders; canoes may not.

• Canoe sprint races are held over 500 m, 1,000 m and 10,000 m for men and 500 m and 5,000 m for women.

• Courses for 500 m and 1,000 m races are straight and competitors must remain in their allotted lanes. Longer races may be divided into a combination of straights and turns, which are marked by red and yellow flags; participants may leave their lanes as long as they do not impede any opponent. There is no penalty in such races if boats touch, as long as no advantage is gained by doing so. Courses with turns are always raced in an anticlockwise direction.

• Competitive canoes and kayaks are classified by a C for Canadian canoe or by a K for kayak, followed by a number that designates the number of persons in the craft: C1, C2 and C4, or K1, K2 and K4.

DIMENSIONS OF VESSELS

Type	Maximum length	Minimum beam	Minimum weight
K1	5.2 m	51 cm	12 kg
K2	6.5 m	55 cm	18 kg
K4	11 m	60 cm	30 kg
C1	5.2 m	75 cm	16 kg
C2	6.5 m	70 cm	20 kg
C4	11 m	75 cm	30 kg

GOVERNING BODY

International Canoe Federation
Calle de la Antracita 7
4º floor
E 28045 Madrid
Spain

E-mail: message@canoeicf.com

Cricket

Cricket began in England in the Middle Ages. King
Edward I (ruled 1272–1307) played a game called *creag*. In
the 18th and 19th centuries, it spread across the British
Empire. Today's leading cricketing nations are Australia,
England, India, New Zealand, Pakistan, South Africa, Sri
Lanka, West Indies and Zimbabwe.

CLOTHING AND EQUIPMENT

- White boots, socks, trousers, shirts and sweaters
  (sweaters may have team colours as a trim)
- Coloured team strips are worn in some one-day
  professional games
- Batsmen and wicketkeepers wear gloves and pads
  that cover the front of their legs
- Most batsmen and close fielders (particularly at short
  leg) wear helmets, sometimes with face-guards
- Wickets: two sets, each 9 in wide, consisting of three
  wooden stumps with two wooden bails on top; the
  stumps are 28 in high and of equal and sufficient size
  to prevent the ball from passing between them; the
  bails are each 4⅜ in long
- Ball: red leather with a stitched seam; circumference
  8–9 in; weight 5½–5¾ oz
- Bat: wooden; maximum length 3 ft 2 in; maximum
  width 4¼ in

CRICKET FIELDING POSITIONS

1 bowler
2 wicketkeeper
3 first slip
4 second slip
5 third slip
6 gully
7 silly point
8 short extra
9 short mid-off
10 silly mid-off
11 silly mid-on
12 short mid-on
13 forward short-leg
14 backward short-leg
15 leg-slip
16 mid-on
17 mid-wicket

18 square-leg
19 short fine-leg
20 short third-man
21 point
22 cover point
23 mid-off
24 deep mid-off
25 long-off
28 deep mid-wicket
29 deep square-leg
30 long leg
31 deep fine-leg
32 deep third-man
33 third-man
34 deep point
35 extra-cover
36 deep-extra

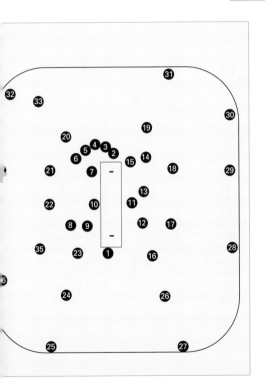

FIELD OF PLAY

A cricket field or ground may be of any size. The distance between the wickets is 22 yd (*see* diagram).

RULES

• A cricket match is played between two sides, each of eleven players.

• The duration of a cricket match may vary. Many games are limited to a single innings per side with a specified number of overs each. Most first-class matches are now played over four days, but Test matches (internationals) are of five days' duration. A playing day is usually six hours long with intervals for lunch (about 40 minutes) and tea (about 20 minutes).

• Matches consist of one or two innings per team. An innings is completed when ten of the batting side have been dismissed, or when the captain of the batting side declares (declares the innings closed), or when the previously agreed number of overs per side has been bowled.

• A new ball is normally taken at the start of each innings or during any innings of more than 75 overs.

• In two-innings matches and some single-innings games, the side with the greater number of runs wins the game, provided that all the opposition wickets have been taken;

if not, the game is a draw. In limited overs games, the side
with more runs is the winner, regardless of how many of
the opposition's wickets it has taken.

- Scoring is in runs. One run is scored when both batsmen,
  after a hit or at any other time when the ball is in play,
  pass each other and reach the opposite popping crease.

- If the ball is hit to the boundary without bouncing, it
  counts six runs; if it reaches the boundary but touches
  the ground on its way, four runs are scored.

- Extras are runs scored without hitting the ball with the
  bat. Wides are runs awarded to the batting side if the
  bowler bowls a ball which, in the umpire's opinion,
  the batsman could not have reached from his natural
  guard position.

- Byes are runs scored when the ball is not fielded quickly
  enough by the wicketkeeper after it has been bowled but
  not hit by the striker, and the batsmen have time to run
  to the opposite popping creases.

- If the ball comes off the batsman's body (but not his bat
  or forearm) unintentionally while he is trying to play a
  stroke, and the ball is diverted far enough from the
  fielders that the batsmen may cross, such runs are 'extras'
  known as 'leg byes'. A no-ball is also an 'extra'.

- In a two-innings match, the teams normally bat
  alternately. However, if the side batting second is all out

after scoring fewer runs than its opponents, it may be asked to follow on, i.e. to take its second innings straightaway, out of turn. The follow-on may be enforced if the team batting second scores 200 less than the opposition in a five-day match, 150 less in a four-day match or 100 less in a two-day match.

- The captain who wins the toss decides whether his team will bat or bowl first. Play begins when all the fielders are in position, the two batsmen have taken up their positions at either wicket, and a bowler bowls to one of them.

- The bowler bowls six balls in an over, after which the next over is bowled from the other wicket. Bowlers may bowl from either end but they must not bowl two consecutive overs. A no-ball is called by the umpire if the bowler throws the ball (it should be delivered with a straight arm) or if, at the moment he releases the ball, the bowler has no part of his front foot behind the popping crease (*see* diagram). If a no-ball is called, the bowler has to bowl an extra ball. Each over must contain six legitimate deliveries.

- A batsman may be out in ten ways:

- Bowled: a batsman is out bowled when the ball delivered by the bowler dislodges a bail, even if the ball touches the batsman or his bat first.

- Caught: a batsman is out caught if the ball touches his bat or if it touches below the wrist his hand or glove, holding the bat, and is subsequently held by a fieldsman before it touches the ground. For a catch to be fair, the fieldsman must not be over, or in contact with, any part of the boundary line. A batsman cannot be caught out if the ball lodges in a fieldsman's protective helmet.

> When the fielders want the umpire to adjudicate on a decision, they appeal to him by shouting 'How was that?', to which the reply is 'Out' or 'Not out'. The cry almost always emerges as 'Owzat?'

- Leg before wicket (LBW): a batsman is out LBW if he first intercepts with any part of his person a fair ball which would have hit the wicket and which has not previously touched his bat or a hand holding the bat. this is providing that the ball is pitched in a straight line between wicket and wicket or on the off side of the wicket (the side of the playing field to the right of a right-handed batsman or the left of a left-hander), or is intercepted before it has bounced and the point of impact is in a straight line between wicket and wicket, even if above the level of the bails. In addition, the batsman is out LBW even if the ball is intercepted outside the line of the off-stump (the stump furthest away from the batsman's legs as he prepares to receive the bowling), if, in the opinion of the umpire, he has made no genuine attempt to play the ball with his bat, but has intercepted the ball with some part of his person

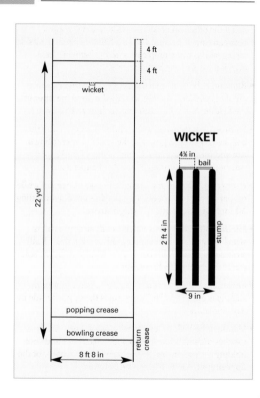

4 ft

4 ft

wicket

WICKET

4⅜ in

bail

2 ft 4 in

stump

22 yd

9 in

popping crease

bowling crease

return crease

8 ft 8 in

and if the other circumstances set out above apply. A batsman cannot be out LBW to a ball that pitched outside his leg-stump (the stump closest to the batman's legs), even if it would have hit the wicket.

- Run out: either batsman (striker or non-striker) is run out if his wicket is broken with the ball by a member of the fielding side while the batsman is out of his crease.

- Stumped: a batsman is out stumped if, in receiving the ball, he is out of his ground other than in attempting a run and the wicket is put down by the wicketkeeper without the intervention of another fieldsman.

- Hit wicket: a batsman is out if he breaks his wicket while preparing to receive a delivery, playing a stroke or setting off for his first run after playing a stroke.

- Hit the ball twice: a batsman is out if, after the ball is struck or stopped by any part of his person, he wilfully strikes it again with his bat or person except for the sole purpose of guarding his wicket.

- Obstructing the field: either batsman (striker or non-striker) is out if he wilfully obstructs the opposite side by word or action.

- Handled the ball: either batsman is out if he wilfully touches the ball while in play with a hand or hands not holding the bat unless he does so with the consent of the opposing side or in order to avoid injury.

- Timed out: an incoming batsman is timed out if he wilfully takes over 2 minutes to come to the wicket.

UMPIRE'S SIGNALS

These are the signals used by umpires to convey their decisions to the scorers:

Boundary 4 – by waving the arm from side to side

Boundary 6 – by raising both arms above the head

Bye – by raising an open hand above the head

Dead Ball – by crossing and re-crossing the wrists below the waist

Leg Bye – by touching a raised knee with the hand

No-Ball – by extending one arm horizontally

Out – by raising the index finger above the head. If not out the umpire shall call 'not out'

Short Run – by bending the arm upwards and by touching the nearer shoulder with the fingertips

Wide – by extending both arms horizontally

GOVERNING BODY

Marylebone Cricket Club (MCC)
Lord's Ground
London NW8 8QN

Website: http://www.lords.org.uk

Croquet

Croquet probably developed from the game of
paille-maille, which was played in France during the
17th century.

CLOTHING AND EQUIPMENT

- White shirts and trousers, shorts or skirts
- Flat sports shoes with smooth soles
- Six hoops: wire wickets 12 in high and 3¾ in wide
- One peg: 1½ in thick, 18 in high
- Mallets: usually wooden; any length; parallel and
  identical end faces
- Four balls: weight 1 lb; diameter 3⅝ in; one blue, one
  black, one red, one yellow

FIELD OF PLAY

The playing surface is a level lawn (the court) measuring
approximately 35 x 28 yd. The hoops and pegs are laid
out as shown in the diagram. The hoops are painted white
with the first hoop having a blue top and the last hoop
(rover) a red top.

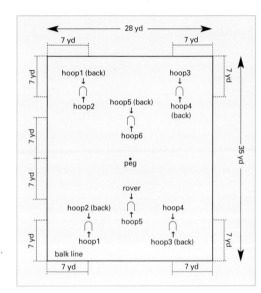

RULES

• Croquet is a game for singles or two teams of two in which mallets are used to drive balls through wickets (also called hoops) in a prescribed sequence. The game is played with four wooden balls: one player or team has blue and black, the other red and yellow. The balls are struck with (usually wooden) mallets that must have identical and parallel faces at either end.

- The object of the game is to drive balls through hoops with the face of the mallet in the order and directions shown in the diagram. The first side to get both its balls through all six hoops twice in order and hit the peg is the winner. Once a ball has completed the circuit and hit the peg (pegged out) it is removed from the game.

- Players take alternate turns starting from the balk line. A player can play either of his balls but must thereafter strike only that ball (the striker's ball) during that turn. A turn consists of a single stroke, unless the ball goes completely through a hoop or hits an opponent's ball (makes a roquet). In the first case, the player gets one more stroke (a continuation stroke); in the second, he gets two more. In the first of these, he places his ball against the ball he has just hit; in the second, he strikes his own ball, ensuring that both balls move.

- A turn ends when a player fails to pass through a wicket or hit an opponent's ball.

- If the striker's ball causes another ball to run through a hoop, that other ball is said to be 'peeled' through the hoop and it gains a point but not a continuation stroke.

- If a ball rolls off the court, it should be replaced on the boundary line at the point where it came off.

- A point is scored every time a ball passes through a hoop and when the ball is pegged out; the winner thus scores 26 points in all.

GOVERNING BODY

The Croquet Association
The Hurlingham Club
Ranelagh Gardens
London SW6 3PR

E-mail: caoffice@croquet.org.uk

Darts

Darts has grown from its roots as an old English pub game into an international sport played by highly rewarded professionals.

CLOTHING AND EQUIPMENT

- No dress code; sartorially almost anything goes
- Dartboard: circular; 1 ft 5¾ in diameter; hung on wall 7 ft 9¼ in from thrower; bull's-eye 5 ft 8 in above the floor
- Darts: maximum length 12 in; maximum weight 1⅛ oz

FIELD OF PLAY

A toe-line known as the oche (pronounced 'ocky') from which players throw their darts at the board.

RULES

THE SIX-DART CHECKOUT

Good players may score 301 in only 6 darts: 3 treble 20s (180), treble 19, 14, and a bull's-eye.

- Players take turns to throw three darts at the target, a board made of cork, bristle or elm and divided by wires into different scoring areas (*see* diagram overleaf).

- Each player or team starts with the same number of points: usually 301, 501, 601, 801 or 1,001. The winner is the first to reduce his score to zero, or check out.

- After each player has thrown three darts, he adds up his score and subtracts the total from his starting score. He then removes his darts and marks his score on a board before the opponent throws.

- Darts that bounce off or miss the board do not score and cannot be re-thrown in that turn.

- To win, a player must reach exactly zero, and the dart that brings the score down to zero must be a double. Doubles are the numbers in the outside narrow scoring band and the centre bull's-eye, which counts as 50 points and is a double of the outer 25-point bull. (Darts that

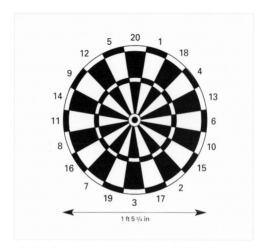

1 ft 5 ¾ in

land in the other narrow scoring band, halfway between the bull's-eye and the doubles, score three times the number shown. The area is known as the treble.)

• At the end of a game, if you have 10 points left, you must hit a double 5 to bring the score down to zero. From 8 points, a double 4 would work. If you have an odd number left, then darts must be thrown to reduce the score to an even number before throwing at a double. For instance, there is no possible double out from 17, so a way to finish would be to throw a single 1 first, reducing the score to 16, then to hit a double 8.

• If a player scores more than he needs to check out, on his next turn his score reverts to what it was before he went bust.

• In some games, players must also start with a double (any double). Each player's scoring begins with the score of the first dart that hits a double.

GOVERNING BODY

British Darts Organisation Ltd
2 Pages Lane
London N10 1PS

Website: http://www.bdodarts.com

Diving

Diving developed as a sport in Europe during the 19th century, and the first competitions took place in England in about 1880. Men first dived in the Olympics in 1904, and women in 1912.

CLOTHING AND EQUIPMENT

• One-piece costume

FIELD OF PLAY

In all sanctioned competitions, diving is done from either a springboard or a platform (highboard). A springboard is bouncy, has an adjustable fulcrum and is 1 m or 3 m above the water surface. The platform is inflexible and stands 5–10 m above the surface. For Olympic and other major competitions for both men and women, the 3 m springboard and 10 m platform heights are used.

Although there are more than 70 different dives, each falls into one of six basic categories, as follows.

Forward: The body faces the water on takeoff and rotates in the same direction.

Back: The body faces the board but rotates towards the water.

Reverse: The body faces the water but rotates back towards the board.

Inward: The body faces the board and rotates in the same direction.

Twist: The body spirals laterally, that is, rotates around its long axis.

Armstand: This dive begins with the competitor standing upside down at takeoff. It is performed from platforms only.

RULES

- Swimmers leap from above the water surface, execute body motions in the air, and enter the pool head or feet first.

- Every dive has four components: the run, the takeoff, the execution, and the entry into the water. These aspects are the only ones judged in competition.

- The execution takes place in the air and consists of one or more of four basic body positions: layout (body straight, legs extended); pike (body bent at waist, legs straight); tuck (legs against chest, hands holding shins); and free (position changing, as in most twisting dives).

- Competitions are usually of two or three rounds, during which each diver must perform both compulsory and optional dives. The former are relatively easy, while the latter – which are chosen by the divers themselves – may be of extraordinary difficulty.

- Diving competitions have five or seven judges who each award a mark from 0 to 10 for each dive. The secretary then cancels the highest and lowest marks, adds up the others, and multiplies the total by a previously determined factor that reflects the degree of difficulty of the dive. In a seven-judge competition, the result is multiplied by three-fifths.

- The diver with the most points in the final round is the winner. If two or more final scores are level, it is a tie.

GOVERNING BODY

Fédération Internationale de Natation Amateur (FINA)
Ave de l'Avant-Poste 4
1005 Lausanne
Switzerland

Website: http://www.fina.org

> The greatest number of Olympic diving medals won is five: Klaus Dibiasi of Italy took three gold and two silver between 1964 and 1976.

Dressage

Dressage tests the docility and physique of the horse, the skill of the rider and the rapport between the two. It is a sport in its own right as well as being one of the components of the **Three-day Event**.

CLOTHING AND EQUIPMENT

- Armed services: military uniform with a helmet or hard hat
- Civilians: dark coat, white breeches, top hat
- Spurs and hunting stock permitted; whips are not allowed
- Horse: over 14.2 hands (1.4 m)

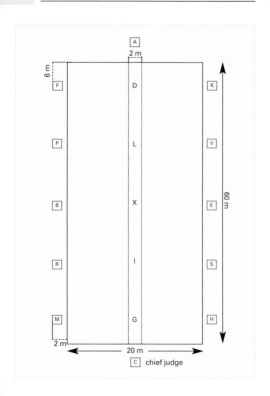

FIELD OF PLAY

Dressage competitions are held on perfectly level sand arenas measuring 60 m x 20 m. Various parts of the arena are marked with letters of the alphabet. It is here that various specified tests must be carried out.

RULES

- The dressage begins when the judges call the competitor, who enters the arena at a trot or a canter. The rider halts, salutes, then attempts to carry out the whole test in a prescribed order from memory.

- If the test requires a movement to be carried out at a particular point of the arena, it must be executed when the rider's body is directly over that marked point.

- A bell is rung whenever the competitor departs from the prescribed direction or pace. The test must then be re-started from the point where the error occurred.

- A fall by horse or rider does not result in elimination. The competitor is penalised only insofar as the fall affects his execution of the test.

- At the end of the test, the competitor salutes again and leaves the arena at the point marked A.

- Each error is penalised 2 points the first time it occurs, 4 points if it is repeated and 8 points the third time. If the error happens a fourth time, the competitor is eliminated.

- Among the test requirements are the halt, the walk, the trot, the canter and the rein back (where the horse goes backwards). The horse and rider may also be expected to turn a quarter circle of approximately 3 m or 6 m radius, depending on the speed at which they are required to be travelling at the time.

> Lippizaners are show horses originally bred and trained at the Spanish Riding School in Vienna, Austria. The breed is noted for its ability to perform the intricate movements of haute école, a discipline of dressage now taught only in the UK. Most Lippizaners are greys.

- Another test, the piaffe, is like a trot on the spot. This should be energetic yet graceful, supple and cadenced.

- There are five judges, three of whom sit on the long side of the arena, while the other two on the short side. Each judge awards every competitor a mark from 0 to 10.

GOVERNING BODY

Fédération Equestre Internationale
Ave Mon Repos 24
PO Box 157
1000 Lausanne 5
Switzerland

Website: http://www.horsesport.org

Fencing

Once only a form of combat, fencing became a sport in the 14th century. It has been an event at every modern Olympic Games since 1896.

CLOTHING AND EQUIPMENT

- Face mask, padded jacket, glove, plastron (protective undergarment)
- Clothing: white and made of strong material; its surface must not be so smooth that the point of an opponent's weapon may glance off it
- Foil: maximum weight 500 g; total length 110 cm; blade 90 cm
- Epée: same length as foil but with larger handguard, stiffer, triangular blade; maximum weight 770 g
- Sabre: overall length 105 cm; blade 88 cm; maximum weight 500 g; handguard has one section attached to pommel at back of handle

FIELD OF PLAY

The playing area is a 'strip' or 'piste', 14 m long and 2 m wide. Matches begin with both fencers standing 2 m apart over the on-guard line at the centre of the piste.

RULES

- The modern foil developed from the short dress-sword introduced in the late 17th century at the court of King Louis XIV of France. Touchés are scored with the point of the blade and must land on the opponent's torso between the neckband of the fencer's uniform and the hipline, groin and back.

- The épée resembles the old duelling sword. Touchés are scored with the point of the blade and the entire body is a valid target area.

- The sabre is a sword with cutting edges along the entire front edge and one-third of the back edge. Touchés may be scored with the point as well as the length of the blade, and the target area includes the front and back torso, arm, hand, neck and head.

- Electric judging equipment is now used in all fencing matches. For foil and épée, a spring-loaded tip is attached to the point of the weapon and connected to a wire that runs inside the blade, through the sleeve of the contestant's jacket and into a central scoring machine that registers hits. In the sabre, a sensor in the handguard is connected to the scoring machine.

- Each time a fencer scores a touch, a point is gained. The objective is to be the first to score five touches on the opponent. Men's bouts are 6 or 10 minutes long, women's 8 minutes. Fencers are warned when there is only 1 minute left. If scores are equal at the end of a bout, a deciding hit is fenced.

> In sabre and foil fencing, each hit must follow the prescribed movements – these are known as the phrase.

- Bouts are officiated by a president, sometimes with the assistance of a number of judges. The president starts play by calling '*En garde*'. He then asks the competitors if they are ready, then calls '*Allez*'.

- Bodily contact (*corps à corps*) is allowed in épée, as long as there is no excessive violence, but forbidden in the other two disciplines, where it is punished first by a warning and then by a penalty of one hit. If fencers go over the sidelines or the rear limits of the piste, they are first warned and then penalised 1 point. Dishonest or brutal play is punished first by a warning, then by the deduction of a point and, finally, by disqualification.

GOVERNING BODY

Fédération Internationale d'Escrime
Ave Mon-Repos 24
Case postale 128
CH1000 Lausanne 5
Switzerland

Website: http://www.fie.ch

Football

Football is the most popular sport in the world. It is also probably one of the oldest, although it was not fully codified until about the time of the first English FA Cup in 1872. The game really established itself with the formation in 1888 of the English Football League.

CLOTHING AND EQUIPMENT

- Outfield players: team strip with numbers on the backs of their jerseys; long socks; shinpads compulsory
- Boots with rubber bars or rounded studs, maximum length ¾ in; minimum diameter ½ in
- Goalkeepers: strips must be of different colours from those of both their own side and the opposition; goalkeepers often wear gloves
- Ball: leather or rubber; round; circumference 27–28 in; weight 15 oz when inflated to 12–13 PSI.

FIELD OF PLAY

A pitch measuring 100–130 yd long and 50–100 yd wide, which must always be longer than it is wide (*see* diagram).

The goals are two upright posts equidistant from the corner-flags and 8 yd apart (inside measurement), and joined by a horizontal crossbar, the lower edge of which is 8 ft from the ground. The width and depth of the crossbars should not exceed 5 in. The goalposts and the crossbars shall have the same width. Nets may be attached to the posts, crossbars and ground behind the goals. They should be appropriately supported and so placed as to allow the goalkeeper ample room.

RULES

- Two teams of eleven players attempt to score goals against each other.

- Only the goalkeeper may handle the ball, and then only within the penalty box, an area measuring 18 yd into the field by 44 yd along the goal line. He may not handle it if it has been passed back to him by a member of his own team. The other ten players play the ball using primarily their feet, although any part of the body may be used other than the hands and arms.

- The number of substitutes permitted varies, but in first-class football, four may be nominated and three used. Their names must be given to the referee before kickoff.

- Before a game, the two captains toss a coin. The winner may kick off or choose which end his team will defend in the first half. If he chooses an end, the other side kicks off.

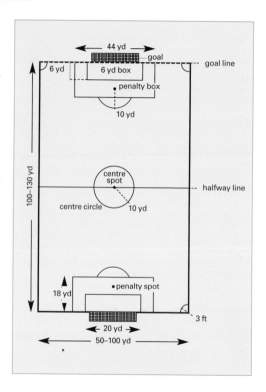

- A game begins when one team kicks off from the centre spot. The first kick must be in a forward direction but the ball must move by no more than its circumference. All subsequent kicks may be any distance or in any direction.

- Play is continuous, stopping only when a goal is scored, the ball is out of bounds, a foul is called, or a player is offside.

- Each match lasts for 90 minutes, 45 minutes each way. The teams change ends at half-time, which now lasts for 15 minutes in professional games.

- The game is controlled by a referee on the field who is assisted by two linesmen, one on each sideline. The main functions of the linesmen are to spot offsides and to indicate which team gets possession when the ball goes out of play.

- Free kicks are awarded for the following offences: intentional contact with the ball with arm or hand (unintentional handball is not unlawful); intentional kicking; charging from behind or in a dangerous manner; striking; holding; pushing and tripping. In each of these cases, the free kick will be direct; in other words, the side to whom the kick is awarded may score directly from it.

- If any of the above offences is committed by a player inside his own team's penalty area, a penalty kick is awarded. The ball is placed on the penalty spot, 10 yd from the goal, and only the goalkeeper may defend. All the other players from both sides must be outside the penalty area and beyond the semicircular line, which has a radius of 10 yd from the spot (*see* diagram).

- If a penalty kick hits the goalposts or crossbar and rebounds into the path of the taker, who then puts it into the net, the goal is disallowed for offside. If, however, after the penalty kick is taken, the ball is parried by the goalkeeper, the taker or any of his team-mates may follow up and score from the rebound.

- Other, lesser offences include obstruction and dangerous play, for which indirect free kicks are awarded within or outside the penalty area; in such cases one pass must be made before a goal can be scored. An indirect free kick is also awarded for offside violations.

- A player is offside if, when the ball is last played by another member of his own team, there are fewer than two opponents nearer than he is to the goal he is attacking. A player may not be offside in his half of the field.

> The word soccer is a contraction and corruption of 'association football'.

- Offside shall not be judged at the moment the player in question receives the ball, but at the moment when the ball is passed to that player by one of his own side.

A player who is not in an offside position when one of his colleagues passes the ball to him does not therefore become offside if he goes forward during the flight of the ball.

> The commonest score in football is 2–1 to the home side.

- A player should not be given offside merely because he is in an offside position. He should be declared offside only if, at the moment the ball touches, or is played by, one of his team, he is interfering with play or with an opponent, or seeking to gain advantage by being in that position.

- A player who is level with the second-last opponent or with the last two opponents is not offside.

- A player cannot be offside if he receives the ball direct from a goal kick, a corner kick or a throw-in.

- A free kick for offside is taken from the spot at which the offence occurred unless it occurred within the opponents' goal area, in which case the kick may be taken from anywhere in the penalty area.

- If the ball is put out of play over the goal line by an attacker, a goal kick is awarded to the defending team. If the ball is put out of play over the goal line by a defender, a corner kick is awarded to the attackers.

- If a player puts the ball out of play along the sidelines, it is put back in by a member of the opposition, who takes a throw-in from the point at which the ball went out. For a throw-in to be legitimate, the following conditions must be satisfied: both the taker's feet must remain on or behind the touchline as the ball is thrown; the ball must be thrown from above and behind the head; the ball must not be dropped; the ball must enter the field of play; the ball must be played by another player before being played again by the player who took the throw.

- If a player commits any of the following offences he may be cautioned (by means of a yellow card, shown by the referee): unsporting behaviour; dissent; persistent offences of any kind; time-wasting; failing to retreat the required distance at corners or free kicks; entering or re-entering the field of play without the referee's permission; deliberately leaving the field of play without the referee's permission.

- If a player commits any of the following seven offences he may be shown a red card and sent off, after which point he may take no further part in the game: serious foul play; violent conduct; spitting at an opponent or any other person; denying the opposing team a goal or an obvious goal-scoring opportunity by deliberately handling the ball; denying an obvious goal-scoring opportunity to an opponent moving towards the player's goal by an offence punishable by a free kick or a penalty kick; using offensive or insulting or abusive language and/or gestures; receiving a second caution in the same match.

GOVERNING BODY

Fédération Internationale de Football Association (FIFA)
FIFA House
PO Box 85
8030 Zürich
Switzerland

Website: http://www.fifa.com

Golf

The earliest recorded mention of golf is in 1457, when the Scottish Parliament banned the game because it distracted men from practising **Archery**.

CLOTHING AND EQUIPMENT

- Dress casual but smart; no jeans or T-shirts
- A glove may be worn on the dominant hand
- Ball: diameter 1.68 in; maximum weight 1⅝ oz
- Clubs: no more than 14 may be carried
- Tees: these are small pegs that are pressed into the ground so that only the top protrudes above the surface. The ball is mounted on a tee for the first shot from each hole.

FIELD OF PLAY

A golf course normally consists of 18 holes. Each hole extends from the teeing ground (or tee) to the hole, which is situated on the putting green (an area of closely cut grass). Between the beginning and end of each hole is a stretch of longer grass known as the fairway. This may contain any number of natural obstacles and manmade bunkers (pits filled with sand). Collectively these are known as hazards. Beyond the fairway is the rough (uncut grass).

RULES

- The object of the game is to play the ball from the tee into each hole in fewer strokes than any opponent.

- There are two forms of play. Match play is decided by the number of holes won and lost. Stroke play is decided by the number of strokes taken to complete the round.

- The teeing ground is the starting place for the hole; it is defined by two tee-markers.

- The putting green contains a hole 4½ in in diameter and at least 4 in deep.

- Out of bounds is ground on which play is prohibited. A ball is out of bounds when all of it lies out of bounds.

- Loose impediments are defined as natural objects such as stones, leaves and twigs, provided they are not fixed or growing or sticking to the ball.

- Obstructions are man-made objects other than those that define out of bounds or are part of the course as defined by local rules.

- Casual water is any temporary accumulation of water other than dew and frost.

- Ground under repair is any portion of the course so marked and also includes material piled for removal and any hole made by a greenkeeper, even if not so marked.

- Each course has local rules, printed on the scorecard.

- Put an identification mark on your ball; if you can't identify your ball, it's lost.

- Don't ask for advice from anyone but your partner or caddie. Don't give advice to anyone but your partner. Do not play practice strokes during a hole.

- Tee off between the tee-markers and up to two club-lengths behind the front line. If you do not, in match

PAR

Determined by the club committee, par is the score that the best golfers are expected to need to complete a hole or round (18 holes). A player who completes a hole in one under par is said to have scored a birdie; two under par is an eagle; three under par is an albatross. One over par is a bogey.

play your opponent may ask you to replay your stroke; in stroke play you incur a two-stroke penalty and must then play from within the proper area.

- Play the ball as it lies. Do not move, bend or break anything fixed or growing, except in fairly taking your stance or making your swing. Do not press anything down or build a stance.

- If your ball lies in a bunker or a water hazard do not touch the ground before making your downswing.

- The ball must be fairly struck, not pushed or spooned.

- If you play the wrong ball in match play you lose the hole; in stroke play you incur a two-stroke penalty and must then play the correct ball.

- On the putting green, you may repair marks on the line of your putt.

- You may mark, lift and clean your ball on the putting green. Always replace it on the exact spot.

- Always remove the flagstick from the hole before you putt. If when putting your ball strikes the flagstick, in match play you forfeit the hole, in stroke play you lose two strokes.

- If you or your partner or caddie move your ball except as permitted by the rules, or if it moves after you have addressed it, add a penalty stroke and replace your ball.

- If your ball is moved by someone else or another ball, replace it without penalty.

- If a ball struck by you is deflected or stopped by you, your partner or your caddie, in stroke play you incur a two-stroke penalty and must play the ball as it lies; in match play you lose the hole.

- If a ball struck by you is deflected or stopped by someone else, in match play you may play it as it lies or replay the stroke without penalty, whereas in stroke play, you must replay it.

- If a ball struck by you is deflected or stopped by another ball at rest, in match play, no penalty is incurred and the ball is played as it lies; in stroke play you incur a two-stroke penalty if your ball and the other ball were on the putting green before you played.

- You may lift your ball if doing so might assist any other player. You may have any ball lifted if it might interfere with your play or assist any other player.

- You may move loose impediments unless they and your ball are in a hazard. If you touch a loose impediment within one club-length of your ball and your ball moves, the ball must be replaced and (unless your ball was on the putting green) you incur a penalty stroke.

- Check local rules for guidance on immovable obstructions (e.g. roads).

- Movable obstructions (e.g. tin cans) may be moved. If the ball moves in the process, it is replaced without penalty.

- If an immovable obstruction interferes with your stance or swing, you may drop the ball within a club-length of the nearest point of relief not nearer the hole. When dropping, stand erect, hold the ball at shoulder height and arm's length, and drop it.

- If your ball is in casual water, ground under repair or a hole made by a burrowing animal, you may drop without penalty within one club-length of the nearest point of relief not nearer the hole.

- Check local rules to see if a hazard is a water hazard (any sea, lake, pond, river, ditch or open water course) or a lateral water hazard (water behind which the committee has decided that it is impractical to drop a new ball).

- In a water hazard, play the ball as it lies or, under penalty of one stroke, either (a) drop anywhere behind the hazard in a straight line between the hole and the point where the ball crossed the hazard's margin, or (b) play again from where you hit the ball into the hazard.

- If the ball is in a lateral water hazard, in addition to the above options, you may, under penalty of one stroke, drop within two club-lengths of either the point where the ball crossed the hazard's margin or a point on the opposite side of the hazard equidistant from the hole.

- Check local rules to identify course boundaries. If your ball is lost in water or out of bounds, you must play another from where the last shot was played under penalty of one stroke. You are allowed 5 minutes to search for a ball. If you think it is lost you may play a 'provisional ball'. You must state that it is a provisional ball and play it before you search for the original. If the original ball is lost or out of bounds, you must continue with the provisional ball under penalty of one stroke. If the original ball is found, you must continue to play the hole with it and abandon the provisional ball.

- If you believe your ball is unplayable, you may, under penalty of one stroke, (a) drop within two club-lengths of where the ball lies not nearer the hole, (b) drop any distance behind the point where the ball lies along a straight line between the hole and the point where the ball lay, or (c) replay the shot. If your ball is unplayable in a bunker you may proceed under (a), (b) or (c). If you choose (a) or (b), you must drop in the bunker.

GOVERNING BODY

The Royal and Ancient Golf Club
St Andrews
Scotland

Website: http://www.randa.org

Hockey

Hockey – sometimes known as field hockey to distinguish it from **Ice Hockey** – originated in ancient Egypt, Persia and Greece and assumed its present form after it reached western Europe.

CLOTHING AND EQUIPMENT

- Outfield players: shirts and shorts or skirts in their team's colours
- Goalkeepers: strip of a different colour from that of both their own side and the opposition; helmet, legpads, gloves and boots with reinforced toes for kicking
- Ball: leather-covered, usually white; weight 5½–5¾ oz (155–163 g); diameter 2⅞–3⅜ in (7.3–7.7 cm)
- Sticks: wooden with a crook at the end; weight 12–28 oz (340–794 g)

FIELD OF PLAY

A hockey field is 100 yd (91.5 m) long and 60 yd (54.9 m) wide. The centre of the field contains a circle with a 1 yd (92 cm) diameter in which the face-off (called a 'bully') takes place.

At each end of the field is a goal, consisting of two upright poles 7 ft (2.13 m) high and 4 yd (3.66 m) apart, and a crossbar. A net is attached. A semicircular striking area extends for a radius of 16 yd (14.64 m) around the goal. Three straight lines are marked across the pitch, one across the centre line and the other two 25 yd (22.87 m) from each goal line.

RULES

- The object of the game is to score a greater number of goals than the opposition. A goal is scored by hitting the ball into the net from within the striking circle.

- Teams consist of eleven players: five forwards, three halfbacks, two fullbacks, and a goalkeeper. A goalkeeper may stop a shot with his stick or body, while other players may use only their sticks.

- The duration of a hockey match is 70 minutes, 35 minutes each way. Teams change ends at half-time, an interval between 5 and 10 minutes. In the event of an injury, play is suspended and the lost time added on at the end of the second half.

- Players may control the ball only with the flat side of their sticks.

- At the start of each half, one side has possession (which is determined by a toss). All players must be in their own half of the field and the first move at the bully must be to

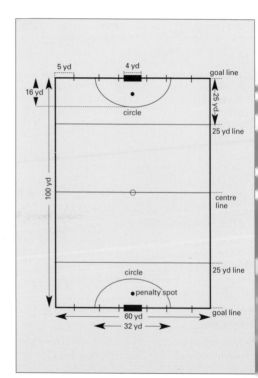

5 yd

4 yd

goal line

16 yd

25 yd

circle

25 yd line

100 yd

centre line

circle

25 yd line

penalty spot

goal line

60 yd

32 yd

play the ball back. Opposing players must be at least 5 yd (4.6 m) from the ball at this and any other free hit.

- After a goal, play is re-started by the team that conceded it.

- When there is a bully to re-start the game after an incident, one player from each team stands squarely facing the sidelines. The ball is placed between them and each then taps his stick first on the ground on his own side of the ball, then on his opponent's stick. This is done three times, after which the players must attempt to strike the ball. A bully must not be played within 16 yd (14.7 m) of the backline or goal line.

- A foul is awarded if a player raises his stick above his shoulder when playing or attempting to play the ball, for tripping, shoving, charging, striking an opponent, playing the ball with the rounded backface of the stick, handling the ball, or for using the stick or a leg deliberately to resist an opponent.

- A player is offside if there are fewer than two opponents within the opposing half when the ball is last played by a team-mate. However, no player may be offside in his own half of the pitch. Offside is penalised only if the team gains an advantage. A free hit is awarded to the opposition from the spot where the offence occurred.

- If the ball crosses the goal line without scoring, the game may be re-started in one of three ways. When the ball was last hit by an attacker or put out of play unintentionally by a defender from more than 25 yd (22.87 m) out, the game re-starts with a free hit from 16 yd (14.7 m). If the ball was put out of play unintentionally by a defender from less

> The first hockey club, Blackheath, was formed sometime before 1861. Because of its popularity in British colonies, particularly in India and Pakistan, Britain and its former possessions have dominated field hockey in the Olympics.

than that distance, a corner is awarded. If a defender intentionally plays the ball over the goal line, a penalty corner is awarded to the attacking team.

- If a player hits the ball out over a sideline, it is put back into play by being placed on the line at the spot where it went over, and pushed or hit by a member of the opposition.

- A penalty corner is awarded for deliberately playing the ball over the backline, for foul play, or for offences within the circle (unless a penalty corner is taken). It is taken from anywhere on the goal line at least 10 yd (9.2 m) from the goalpost. Not more than five defenders are permitted to stand behind their own goal line or backline when a penalty corner is taken. The rest of the defending team must be beyond the centre line.

- A corner hit is taken by an attacker on the backline within 5 yd (4.6 m) of the corner flag. The player who takes it may not, after striking it, remain within playing distance of the ball until it has been played or touched by another player of either team.

- A penalty stroke is awarded against defenders in the circle for an intentional foul, an unintentional foul that prevents a goal, or for persistent and deliberate infringements at penalty corners. The stroke is taken from a spot 7 yd (6.4 m) in front of the middle of the goal by an attacker who may take one step forward to push, flick or scoop the ball. Thereafter he may not hit it again or approach the goal. The goalkeeper must defend this stroke alone, and may not move from his position on the goal line until after the ball has been played. All other players must stand beyond the 25 yd (22.87 m) line. If the goalkeeper illegally prevents a goal, it is still awarded. If no goal is scored, play is re-started with a free hit to the defending side from the 16 yd (14.7 m) line in front of the centre of the goal.

GOVERNING BODY

Fédération Internationale de Hockey

Ave des Arts, 1 bte 5
1210 Brussels
Belgium

Website: http://www.fihockey.org

Ice Hockey

Modern ice hockey began in Canada in the mid-19th century. The first formal game was played in Kingston, Ontario in 1855, with teams drawn from the Royal Canadian Rifles. World and Olympic championships have been held since 1920.

CLOTHING AND EQUIPMENT

- Protective shoulder-, hip- and elbowpads; knee- and shinguards; heavy leather gloves; helmets
- Goaltenders also wear massive leg- and chestpads, gloves and face mask
- Puck: black vulcanised rubber disc; diameter 7.6 cm; thickness 2.5 cm; weight 156–170 g
- Sticks: aluminium shafts with replaceable wooden blades; maximum dimensions: handles 1.4 m long, 3.2 cm wide, 1.9 cm thick; blades 32 cm long, 7.5 cm wide
- Goaltenders' sticks may be wider and heavier
- Skates: short, curved blades to permit quick turns and stops
- Goaltenders' skates have longer, flat blades for stability

FIELD OF PLAY

Rinks vary in size, although standard international dimensions specify a playing area 61 m long and 26 m wide, with corners rounded into the arc of a circle with a 9.2 m radius.

> Ice hockey was institutionalised in North America in 1893, when it was first taken up by the US universities Yale and Johns Hopkins. The first professional ice hockey team was the Boston Bruins, founded in 1924.

The rink is enclosed by retaining boards 1.1–1.2 m high and divided into three zones: two end zones and a neutral zone. The zones are marked on the ice by blue lines. Two red goal lines, 5 cm wide, also run the width of the rink. There is a space of 3.35 m between the goal lines and the barrier boards at each end of the ice.

The two goal cages have openings 1.2 m high and 1.8 m wide, with the posts resting on the goal lines. Around the mouth of the goal is a rectangular area 2.53 m wide and 1.8 m deep, known as the crease, which is marked by red lines 5 cm-wide.

Two blue lines 39 cm-wide extend the width of the ice in the centre of the rink 18.3 m from each goal line. A red line, seen only in professional ice hockey, also 39 cm wide, bisects the length of the rink between the blue lines. The blue lines designate attacking and defending zones, depending on which team controls the puck.

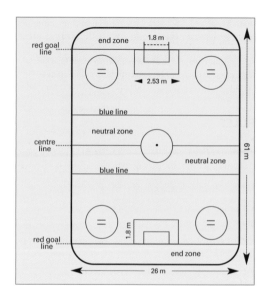

In the centre of the rink is a red spot 30 cm in diameter, around which is marked a circle with a 3 m radius. There are four other spots and circles of the same size, two in each end zone. They are located halfway between each goalpost and the boards and 4.6 m out from the goal lines. In professional hockey, four red spots of the same size are in the neutral zone midway between the boards and the centre of the rink and 1.5 m from each blue line. The centre spot is where play starts at the beginning of each period or after a goal is scored. The other spots are where play is resumed after a stoppage. The team that scores most goals is the winner

RULES

- Ice hockey is played by two teams of six players. Each team consists of a goaltender, two defenders and three forwards (a centre and two wings). Up to twelve substitutes may be used. In the professional leagues, play is supervised by three officials; in amateur games, two officials are used.

- The home team has choice of ends at the start.

- Play consists of three 20-minute periods, each of which starts at the centre spot with a face-off. The official drops the puck, and the two centres try to control it.

- The flow of play in ice hockey is frequently interrupted by offside and icing. A player is offside if he precedes the puck into the attacking zone. This rule prevents players from goal-hanging. If a player is offside, the game is re-started with a face-off at one of the red spots in the neutral zone nearest to where the offence was committed.

- If the puck crosses the centre- and goal-lines without being touched by the opposition, the referee calls 'Icing'

and play is re-started with a face-off in the defensive zone
of the penalised team at the red spot nearest to where the
offence took place.

- Other offences include tripping, holding and hooking,
  or spearing with the stick. For such fouls the offending
  player must leave the game for between 2 and 5 minutes.
  More serious infractions, such as fighting, draw 5- or
  10-minute penalties. The penalised team must play
  shorthanded, while the other team, at full strength,
  enjoys a period of what is known as power-play. The
  penalised player may return if his team concedes a goal
  while he is in the penalty box (on the sidelines).

- In the event of a tie, there is a period of overtime during which the first team to score is the winner. The exact length of overtime may vary, but for amateurs it is usually 10 minutes. If the scores are still level at the end of overtime, the match is tied.

GOVERNING BODY

National Hockey League
1251 Ave of the Americas
New York, NY 10020
USA

Website: http://www.nhl.com

Ice-skating

Ice-skating as a sport developed in the Middle Ages on frozen lakes in Scotland and canals in the Netherlands. The first skating club was founded in Edinburgh in 1742.

CLOTHING AND EQUIPMENT

- Clothing must be modest, dignified, warm, comfortable and allow freedom of movement
- Skates: single steel blade approximately 3 mm wide

FIELD OF PLAY

Modern ice-skating competitions are held on rectangular rinks which are 56–60 m long and 26–30 m wide. Live music or a sound system must be provided, because all events are accompanied by music.

> The earliest ice-skating blades were made of first of animal bone and then of wood. The English word 'skate' is derived from the Dutch word *schaats*, meaning 'leg bone' or 'shank bone'. From 1572 skates began to be made of iron, which reduced both friction and lateral slipping.

RULES

- Artistic ice-skating competitions are divided into a number of different events within three main categories: solo skating, pair skating, and ice-dancing.

- In both singles and pairs competitions, contestants go on to the ice twice. First they perform an original programme featuring eight prescribed elements with connecting steps. The latter should be kept to a minimum, and points are deducted if additional elements are added. Later they return to do a free routine comprising movements of their own choice. Marks out of 6 are awarded for technical merit (composition) and artistic impression (presentation).

- For original programmes the maximum duration is 2 minutes 40 seconds. Skaters may finish sooner if they have completed all the required moves, but no extra marks may be obtained for extending the programme or repeating moves that have failed.

- There is a draw to decide the starting order in the compulsory section. In subsequent sections it is determined by the competitors' previous performance.

- For free-skating, the maximum times are 4½ minutes for men, 4 for women. Skaters must finish within 10 seconds before or after the specified time. The end of the time is signalled by a gong or whistle.

- In pairs skating, each couple must be one man and one woman. They need not always remain in contact and their movements need not be identical, but they must present a united, harmonious performance.

- Partners may not be carried for more than three complete revolutions. The arm of the lifter must be fully extended.

- The following movements are forbidden: lifting with anything other than the hands; holding the partner's legs; swinging the woman while holding her hand or foot; turning the lifted partner in a horizontal position; jumping towards the other partner; rotating with one partner holding the other's leg, arm or neck.

- Ice-dancing, which is also for couples, consists of three programmes: compulsory, free and original. The compulsory section must contain two dances from two of the following three groups:

  - Westminster Waltz; Viennese Waltz; Starlight Waltz; Ravensberger Waltz

  - Kilian; Quickstep; Paso Doble; Yankie Polka

  - Blues; Rhumba; Argentine Tango; Tango Romantica

- Free dancing consists of non-repetitive combinations of dance movements in a 4-minute programme. Competitors choose their music and all their own steps, turns and changes of position, provided they conform to committee rules. Marks are awarded for expertise and ability in dancing, as well as for originality of ideas.

- The original dance is treated as a separate event. Each couple chooses its music, tempo and composition, but the rhythm is decided annually by committee. The dance consists of sequences that complete a circuit of the rink.

GOVERNING BODY

International Skating Union
Chemin de Primerose 2
CH1007 Lausanne
Switzerland

Website: http://www.isu.org

Lacrosse

Lacrosse was first played by native North American tribes, and games were sometimes 200-a-side. European settlers took it up and the laws were codified in 1867.

CLOTHING AND EQUIPMENT

- Gloves; helmets with face masks, chin straps and sometimes eye-, mouth- and nose-guards.
- Each team's jerseys should be of the same colour, and have numbers on chest and back
- Sticks (crosses): short crosse 40–42 in, long crosse 52–72 in; apart from the goalkeeper's crosse, only four long crosses per team; the head of the crosse is 4–10 in at its widest point and has a net attached to it
- Ball: white, yellow or orange solid rubber; diameter 7¾–8 in; weight 5–5¼ oz

FIELD OF PLAY

Modern men's lacrosse is a ten-a-side game played on a field measuring 110 x 60 yd.

There are two goals measuring 6 ft x 6 ft with pyramid-shaped nets. The goals are placed 15 yd from each end line inside a circle (the goal crease) with a diameter of 6 yd.

RULES

• A match is usually divided into 4 periods of 20 minutes, between which there are intervals of 2, 10 and finally 3 minutes. Teams change ends after each quarter.

• In the event of a tie, two 4-minute periods of overtime may be played, after which, if the scores remain level, the match is decided by sudden death, in which further 4-minute periods are played (after each of which the teams again change ends) until a goal is scored.

• Teams comprise a goalkeeper, three defenders, three midfielders and three attackers. Up to 13 substitutes may be used.

- Each goal counts 1 point. The ball may be carried, thrown or batted with the crosse. The goalkeeper alone may handle the ball, but only within his own crease, and even there he may not catch it, only deflect it.

- Choice of goals is determined by a toss. Play begins with a face-off . One player from each team stands in the middle of the centre line facing the other on either side of the ball. The referee calls 'Are you ready? Play' then blows his whistle, whereupon both players try to play the ball with their crosses. The players in the wing areas can run after the ball when the whistle sounds, but the others must not move until one player has gained possession of the ball, or the ball has moved out of the central area.

> Women's lacrosse is twelve-a-side. Pitches are usually 120 x 70 yd, but may be any size.

- Centre face-offs are also used to start each quarter and after a goal is scored.

- If the ball or a player with the ball goes out of bounds, the other team is awarded possession and the player who re-starts the game must be given 3 ft of clear space. If the ball goes out of bounds after an unsuccessful shot, possession is awarded to the player nearest the ball when it went out. He re-starts the game with a free play, when all other players must be at least 9 ft from the ball.

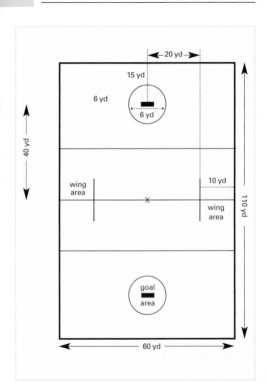

- An attacking player cannot enter the crease around the goal, but may reach in with his stick for a loose ball.

- Bodychecks (takeouts) are permitted, but only on the player with the ball or within 9 ft of a loose ball. Bodychecks must be made from the front or side between neck and hip.

- Fouls are penalised by awarding possession to the opposition at the spot where the infringement occurred. If the opposition already has the ball, the offending player is sent off for 30 seconds. Sent-off players are said to be 'in the box'.

- There are two types of foul. Technical fouls include handling the ball, pushing or holding an opponent or his crosse, wasting time and offside (if a team has fewer than three players in its attacking half of the field and/or fewer than four players in its own half). Personal fouls include illegal bodychecking, reckless swinging of the crosse (slashing), impeding an opponent with the crosse handle (crosse-checking), tripping, and violent and unsportsmanlike conduct. Personal fouls are punishable by loss of possession and/or sendings off, which may last between 1 and 3 minutes. The exact duration of any suspension is at the discretion of the referee.

- Players who commit five personal fouls are fouled out of the game and may take no further part.

GOVERNING BODY

International Lacrosse Federation
Constitution/Rules Committee
7 Kurrajong Place
Greenwood 6024
Western Australia

Website: http://www.intlaxfed.org

Netball

Netball is a seven-a-side game usually played by women.
Up to three substitutes may be permitted. Goals are
scored by sending the ball through a ring at the
opponents' end of the court.

CLOTHING AND EQUIPMENT

- Shirts or blouses with the initials of playing position on chest and back; skirts or shorts; socks and shoes with smooth soles
- No jewellery apart from wedding rings, which must be taped
- Ball: weight 14–16 oz; circumference 1 ft 2 in; a size 5 football ball may be used

---

FIELD OF PLAY

The court should have a hard surface and measure 100 ft long by 50 ft wide. It is divided into thirds of equal length: a goal third at each end and a centre third. In each goal third is marked a semicircle 32 ft in diameter with the goal at its centre. This is known as the shooting circle. In the middle of the court is a circle in which the centre player stands at the start of the game.

Each goalpost must be 10 ft tall; each ring should stand 6 in proud of the post and have a circumference of 1 ft 3 in.

RULES

• Players must pass the ball by throwing it, but they must not run with it. They are restricted to certain areas of the court. The positions are goal shooter, goal attack, wing attack, centre, wing defence, goal defence and goalkeeper. All players must remain within their designated areas (*see* diagram).

• A netball match is divided into 4 quarters of 15 minutes each. Half-time is the mean average requested by the teams up to a maximum of 10 minutes. The two breaks between quarters are each 3 minutes long.

• Time is added on at the end of each quarter in which an injury occurs.

• The captains toss for choice of ends or the first centre pass.

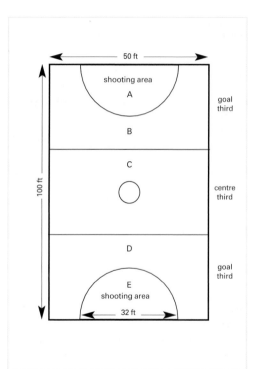

- The game is started by the centre, who must pass the ball within 3 seconds of the starting whistle. The defending centre may not come within 3 ft of the other centre and all the other players must be within their own areas until the whistle is blown. The first pass must go to a player who moves to arrive in the centre third of the court.

- Shots may be attempted at goal only from within the shooting circle and goals may be scored only by goal shooters or goal attacks. Own goals may be scored if the ball goes through the ring after a defender has attempted to intercept a shot at goal.

- If one side puts the ball out of play along the sides of the court, it is put back by a throw-in taken by the opposition. The throw must be taken within 3 seconds of the player receiving the ball.

- If it is impossible to determine which team put the ball out of play, the game is re-started by the umpire tossing the ball up between two players opposite where the ball went out.

- Players may catch the ball in one hand or both hands or deflect it to another player. They may throw or bounce the ball to another player. No player may hold the ball for longer than 3 seconds.

- Players may not roll the ball, run with it, throw it in the air and catch it again, bounce it, or drop it and pick it up.

They may not deliberately kick it, grab it from an opponent, punch it, or play the ball while they are on the ground.

- Players must not use the goalpost as a means of support, nor pull at it to keep a shot out of the ring.

- All passes must be made over a distance large enough to permit a third player to pass between the passer and the intended recipient.

- A pass may not be thrown over a whole third of the court without being touched by a player in that third.

- A player may not move with the first foot grounded after catching the ball, but may move the other foot in any direction any number of times within the 3-second time limit. Pivoting on a foot does not count as a step. Hopping is not allowed.

Players on the team playing towards the goal at the top of the diagram may occupy the following areas only:

Goal shooter	A	B			
Goal attack	A	B	C		
Wing attack		B	C		
Centre		B	C	D	
Wing defence			C	D	
Goal defence			C	D	E
Goalkeeper				D	E

- No player, with or without the ball, may come into contact with an opponent in such a manner as to interfere with her play.

- Any player coming closer than 3 ft of another player is guilty of obstruction. The penalty for obstruction is a penalty pass if the offence is committed outside the circle, or the option of a penalty pass or a penalty shot if the offence is committed inside the circle. In either case, the offender must stand beside the thrower and take no part in the play until the ball has left the thrower's hands.

- All other offences are penalised with a free pass from where the infringement took place.

- Players are offside if they go outside the boundaries of their area. They may catch the ball beyond the line but their feet must remain inside it.

GOVERNING BODY

The International Federation of Netball Associations
Birmingham Sports Centre
Highgate
Birmingham B12 9DL

Website: http://www.netball.org

Polo

Polo is thought to have originated in India more than 5,000 years ago. The first written account describes a game between the Persians and the Turkomans in about 600 BC. The name polo comes from *pulu*, the Persian for willow root, the material from which the balls were made. Polo ponies take about four years to train. Most of the best come from Argentina, which has dominated the sport since 1945. The Cup of the Americas, between Argentina and the USA, is considered the world's premier polo tournament. It is not held regularly, but occurs when either country decides to mount a challenge.

CLOTHING AND EQUIPMENT

- Each team plays in a uniform colour or colours
- Helmets or caps with chinstrap
- Boots and kneepads with no buckles or studs
- No sharp spurs
- Ball: white; traditionally ash, bamboo root or willow, now often plastic; diameter 3¼ in; weight 3½–4½ oz
- Ponies: regardless of their size, which is unrestricted, polo horses are always known as ponies
- Mallet: may be of any length or weight. The mallet heads are covered in ash, bamboo, sycamore or vellum (the skin of a calf or a kid)

FIELD OF PLAY

Polo is played on the largest pitch of any sport with a maximum length of 300 yd and a maximum width of 200 yd. The field is enclosed by wooden sideboards 11 in high which keep the ball in play.

The goals are two poles 10 ft high with flags on top of them. There is no crossbar.

RULES

- Two teams of four mounted horsemen attempt to drive a small wooden ball through the opposing team's goalposts with a special mallet.

- A goal is scored when the ball is driven between the posts. They are imagined to extend upwards to infinity, so the height at which the ball passes through them is immaterial.

- The game is usually divided into four to eight periods, known as chukkers or chukkas, of 7 minutes each. Ends are changed at half-time and after every goal, unless the goal was scored from a penalty.

- Play begins at the T-shaped mark in the centre of the field. Each team lines up on its own side of the halfway mark. The umpire bowls the ball underarm between the two ranks of players at a distance of not less than 5 yd.

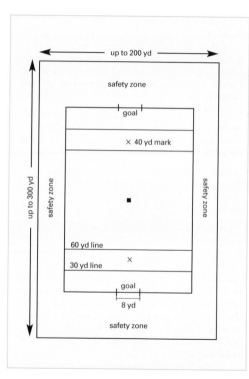

- The ball is out of play if it goes over the perimeter boards. If it goes out along the sides, it is put back in by the umpire, who rolls it back from the spot at which it went out. If a defender puts it out of play at the back, play is re-started with a penalty hit to the attacking team from the 60 yd line opposite the point at which the ball went out.

- If the ball is damaged or becomes lodged in a player's clothing, play is re-started by its being bowled to the nearer side of the ground at least 20 yd from the goal and the sidelines.

- Penalties for various offences are assessed by two mounted officials and may include free goals and free shots at the goal, depending on the severity of the offence under discussion.

- There are two forms of penalty hit: from 30 yd or 60 yd. The former is taken from a spot opposite the goal. The offending side must remain behind the backline until the ball has been hit and may not stand behind the goal or ride out between the goalposts. Alternatively, the captain of the team to which the penalty has been awarded may opt to take the hit from the spot where the foul occurred (but at least 4 yd from the sidelines, in which case no member of the opposition may be within 30 yd of the ball. The other players in the side taking the hit must all be behind the ball.

- The 60 yd penalty is also taken from a spot opposite the middle of the opponents' goal. The attackers may position themselves where they wish; the defenders must be at least 30 yd from the ball.

- The most important principle of polo is right of way, which belongs to the player or players following the exact line of the ball as closely as possible. If the ball comes to a standstill, the line is deemed to be an extension of the direction in which it was travelling before it stopped.

- If two players are approaching the ball from different angles, the player with the ball on his right side has right of way. No player may hit the ball on his left side.

GOVERNING BODY

The Hurlingham Polo Association
Manor Farm
Little Coxwell
Faringdon
Oxon SN7 7LW

Website: http://www.hpa-polo.co.uk

Rounders

Rounders is an English game similar to **Baseball** and
softball. The earliest recorded matches date from the 16th
century. Today it is played mainly by women and children.

CLOTHING AND EQUIPMENT

- Shirts or blouses, shorts or skirts
- Footwear may have studs up to 30 mm in
  circumference; no spikes
- Bat: round; wood, aluminium or plastic; maximum
  length 46 cm; maximum circumference 17 cm
- Ball: white leather; circumference 18–20 cm; weight
  70–85 g
- Four bases: vertical posts 1.2 m high

FIELD OF PLAY

Rounders may be played on grass, asphalt or any surface
suitable for running on, but mixed surfaces are not
allowed. The playing field is marked out with four bases.
The batting square and the first three posts (first base,
second base and third base) should be laid out in a square
with a side of 12 m. Fourth base should be 8.5 m from
third base (*see* diagram).

RULES

- The game is played between two teams of at least six and no more than 15 players. There may be no more than nine on the pitch at any time. No more than five males are allowed in mixed teams.

- One team bats, the other fields. Players take it in turns to hit the ball and then run round the track past all four bases to score rounders. The bowler bowls underarm from a line 7.5 m from the batting square.

- A match consists of two innings. A team which is five or more rounders behind after the first innings bats again, and if it fails to overtake the opposition's single innings score, the game is over.

- A no-ball is a delivery which is higher than the batter's head, lower than his knee, too wide for him to reach, aimed at the non-hitting side of his body, or which bounces before it reaches the batter. The bowler must have both feet within the bowling square when the ball is released.

- A batter may choose to play a no-ball; if he does so, he cannot be caught out off it.

- A rounder is scored if a batter hits the ball and runs round all four bases without stopping before the ball can be returned to the bowler. A half-rounder is scored if he hits the ball and reaches second base or runs all the way

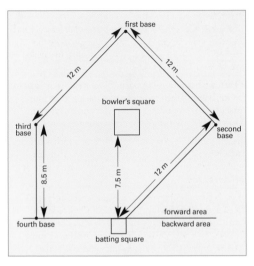

round without having hit the ball. A penalty half-rounder is scored if the bowler delivers two consecutive no-balls to a batter, or if a fielder obstructs the batter while he is taking strike or on his way round the bases.

• If the batter hits the ball behind him into the backward area, he may not run beyond first base until it is returned into the playing zone. However, he may run as soon as it does so, and it is therefore possible to score a rounder off a ball played behind the back stop.

- Each batter is entitled to one good ball only. Having hit the ball, attempted to hit it, or let it pass, he must then run to at least the first base, carrying the bat with him. Only one batter may be on any post at one time, so all the batters need to run round at the same time.

- If the batter misses a good ball, the back stop will throw the ball to the fielder at first base to try to run him out.

- A batter is out if he is caught; if he fails to keep both feet in the batting square until after he has hit the ball or it has passed him; if a fielder touches the base ahead with the ball before he reaches it; or if he runs inside a base.

- A batter may also be out if, after having reached one of the bases, he lets go of it and the player on the base touches the post with the ball.

- Once played, the ball is not dead until it is returned to the hands of the bowler, who should hold the ball above his head when he receives it. After he has done this, there should be no further movement by any of the batters on the bases until after the next delivery. However, if the bowler fails to catch it, batters may run to another base, even if the ball had previously been gathered by one of the fielders on a base.

GOVERNING BODY

National Rounders Association
55 Westland Gardens
Westfield
Sheffield S20 8ES

E-mail: rounders@nra-rounders.co.uk

Rowing

Rowing as a modern sport developed on the River
Thames. Since 1839 the world's top amateur race has been
the Diamond Sculls, which is rowed over 2112 m annually
at the Henley Royal Regatta.

CLOTHING AND EQUIPMENT

- Shorts and vests, often uniform colour or colours
- Racing boats – known as shells – vary in size
  according to the number of crew members. A
  modern eight-man shell weighs about 91 kg, is
  18.3 m long, and has a very narrow beam (hull
  width) averaging 46 cm. Crew members sit on
  sliding seats mounted on rollers that permit leg
  muscles to be brought into use with each stroke.

FIELD OF PLAY

Most international rowing races are held over 2000 m
courses which are straight, current-free and divided into
lanes. The main exceptions are veterans' events, which are
usually raced over 1000 m. Regattas and head of the river
races may be held over any stretch of river, natural or
artificial lake, or along a coast.

RULES

• There are two categories of race: one for sculls, the
  other for rowing boats. In sculling, the rower holds
  two oars and competes in boats that have one, two or
  four scullers.

- In rowing events a rower holds one oar and is part of a crew of two, four or eight oarsmen. Traditionally, each oar is alternately on the left and right side of the boat. Some boats have a cox (short for coxswain), who sits at the stern of the boat and steers. There are rowing events for coxless pairs, coxed pairs, coxless fours, coxed fours and coxed eights.

> The earliest literary account of rowing as a sport is found in the *Aeneid*, a Latin epic poem by Virgil (70–19 BC) which describes a race at the funeral games in honour of Anchises, the father of the hero, Aeneas.

- There are two categories of rowing event: regattas, which are knockout competitions, and head-of-the-river races, in which boats set off at intervals and are timed over the course.

GOVERNING BODY

Fédération Internationale des Sociétés d'Aviron (FISA)
Ave de Cour 135
Case Postale 18
1000 Lausanne 3
Switzerland

Website: http://www.worldrowing.com

Rugby League

Rugby League began in 1895 when a number of clubs in the north of England broke away from the Rugby Football Union in order to turn professional, as the Union code was at the time staunchly amateur.

CLOTHING AND EQUIPMENT

- Each team has a uniform strip: jerseys with numbers on the back; shorts, long socks and studded boots; shinpads optional
- Ball: oval; leather or synthetic material in four panels; length 28–30 cm; circumference 76–79 cm from end to end, 58–62 cm at widest point; weight 0.4 kg; pressure 0.67–0.70 kg cm^2

FIELD OF PLAY

Grass pitch measuring 100 m from goal to goal and 69 m from touchline to touchline (*see* diagram). The goalposts are H-shaped. The crossbar is 3 m above ground, the uprights 5.5 m apart and no less than 4 m high.

RULES

- Broadly similar to **Rugby Union**, Rugby League is played by two teams of 13 players, with a maximum of four replacements per side.

For 100 years, the Rugby Football Union outlawed all forms of professionalism, and anyone who played Rugby League was banned from Union for life. This all changed with the advent of the open era in the mid-1990s, and players may now play either code with impunity.

- A try is worth 4 points; a conversion or penalty goal scores 2 points; a drop goal is 3 points in England, 1 point elsewhere.

- One of the main differences between **Union** and League is the rule about tackling. In Rugby League a team is allowed to be tackled no more than five times in succession; on the sixth tackle they lose possession to the opposition.

- Until possession is lost, a tackled player is released so that he may play the ball to a team-mate by rolling it backwards under his foot.

- A penalty kick may be a punt, a drop kick or a place kick, unless the kicker is attempting to score, in which case it must be either a drop kick or a place kick.

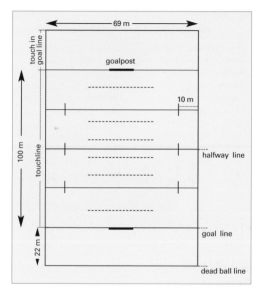

- In professional Rugby League, persistent minor offences may result in a player being suspended for 5 or 10 minutes in the Sin Bin. Serious offences may be punished by sending off the guilty player, who may take no further part in the match.

NUMBERS AND POSITIONS

Although Rugby League Super League players now have personal squad numbers, the traditional numbers and positions are as follows:

Backs		Forwards	
1	fullback	8	prop
2	right wing	9	hooker
3	right centre	10	front row
4	left centre	11	second row
5	left wing	12	second row
6	stand-off half	13	loose forward
7	scrum half		

• The scrum contains six players on each side, who link up in a 3–2–1 formation.

GOVERNING BODY

The Rugby Football League
Red Hall
Red Hall Lane
Leeds LS17 8NB

Website: http://www.rfl.uk.com

Rugby Union

While playing football at Rugby School in 1823, William Webb Ellis picked up the ball in his hands and ran with it. This led to the creation of a new game which was codified in 1871 as Rugby Union.

CLOTHING AND EQUIPMENT

- Each team has a uniform strip: jerseys with numbers on the back; shorts, long socks and studded boots; shinpads optional
- Ball: leather or synthetic material in four panels; oval; length 28–30 cm; circumference 76–79 cm from end to end, 58–62 cm at widest point; weight approximately 0.4 kg; pressure 0.67–0.70 kg cm^2

FIELD OF PLAY

Grass pitch measuring 100 m from goal to goal and 69 m from touchline to touchline (*see* diagram).

RULES

- In Rugby Union, the ball may be kicked or handled but it may not be passed forward. The game is normally played on grass, but may also take place on clay or sand.

- A team consists of 15 players who start the match, plus up to seven replacements and/or substitutes. A team can substitute up to two front-row players and up to five other players. Players who have been sent off may not be replaced.

- A match lasts 80 minutes and is divided into two halves. The teams change ends at half-time, an interval of not more than 10 minutes.

- The kickoff at the start of each half and after a conversion attempt is a place kick taken at the centre of the halfway line. All the kicker's team must be behind the ball. All the opposing team must stand on or behind the 10 m line.

- From the kickoff, the ball must land in the field of play. If it is kicked directly into touch the opposing team may have the kick re-taken, have a scrum at the centre (they have the throw-in) or a line-out on the halfway line.

- A try is scored when an attacking player is first to ground the ball in the opponents' in-goal. It counts 5 points.

A penalty try is awarded between the posts if a player would probably have scored a try but for foul play by an opponent. It scores 5 points.

- When a player scores a try or a team is awarded a penalty goal, the team then attempts to score a conversion by taking a kick at goal from a point in line with the spot at

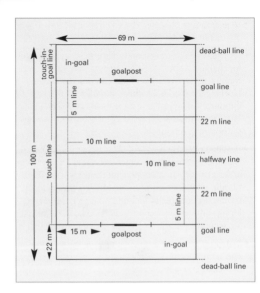

which the try was scored. A conversion kick can be a place kick or a drop kick. It scores 2 points.

- A dropped goal is scored by a player who kicks the ball between the posts and above the crossbar from a drop kick in open play. It scores 3 points.

- A goal cannot be scored directly from a kickoff, a drop-out or a free kick.

- A penalty goal scores 3 points. Penalties may be awarded for charging or pushing other than shoulder-to-shoulder; running in front of a team-mate carrying the ball; blocking the tackler; blocking the ball so as to prevent an opponent from playing it; if the man with the ball runs into a team-mate at a set piece; or if a flanker obstructs the opposing scrum half.

- Penalties may also be awarded for unfair play; time-wasting; throwing the ball into touch; punching, striking, kicking or tripping an opponent; dangerous tackling; playing an opponent without the ball (other than in a scrum, ruck or maul); tackling a jumper in the air; or lifting in the scrum. Players guilty of dangerous play are sent off.

- When a player has been cautioned, the referee will show him a yellow card. When a player is being sent off, the referee will show him a red card.

- If a penalty is awarded in the in-goal area, the kick is taken 5 m back from the goal line in line with the place of infringement.

- A player is offside if he is in front of a team-mate who is carrying the ball or in front of a team-mate who last played the ball. Offside means that a player is temporarily out of the game and a penalty is awarded against him if he takes part in it.

• A knock-on occurs when a player loses possession of the ball and it goes forward, or when a player hits the ball forward with hand or arm, or when the ball hits the hand or arm and goes forward and touches the ground or another player before the original player can catch it. The one exception is if the ball goes forward as in a knock-on when a player charges down an opponent's kick but does not try to catch the ball, in which case play continues.

• If the knock-on is involuntary, a scrum is awarded at the place of infringement. The exceptions are: when it takes place at a line-out, in which case the scrum is awarded 15 m from the touchline; when the ball ends up in-goal, in which case the scrum is awarded where the knock-on happened; or if the knock-on takes place in-goal, in which case a 5 m scrum is awarded in line with the place of the infringement not closer than 5 m to the touchline.

• If the knock-on is intentional, a penalty is awarded to the opposition. If the ball is knocked forward while a player attempts to catch the ball and that player catches the ball before it has touched the ground or another player, play continues.

• A drop-out – a drop kick by the defending team – is used to re-start play after a defender has made the ball dead behind the goal line or it has gone into touch-in-goal or over the dead-ball line. The drop-out may be taken anywhere on or behind the 22 m line. All the kicker's team must be behind the ball.

- If, after a drop-out, the ball does not cross the 22 m line, the opposing team may ask for another drop-out to be taken, or have a scrum at the centre of the 22 m line. They throw in the ball. From the drop-out the ball must land in the field of play. If it is kicked directly into touch, the opposing team may request another drop-out, have a scrum at the centre of the 22 m line (they throw in the ball), or accept the kick. If they accept the kick, the throw-in is where the ball went into touch.

- A player on the ground with the ball must immediately get up with the ball, pass it or release it. If he fails to do one of these things, a penalty is awarded against him.

- A player must not lie on the ball or on another player who has the ball or who is within 1 m of it. A penalty is awarded against players who break this rule.

- A ruck occurs when one or more players from each team, who are on their feet, in physical contact, close around the ball on the ground and use their feet to try to win or keep possession of the ball. Players in a ruck must have their heads and shoulders no lower than their hips and bind onto the ruck with at least one arm around the body of a team-mate. Players in a ruck must try to stay on their feet. They must not voluntarily fall or kneel, jump on the ruck or deliberately collapse it.

- A maul occurs when a player carrying the ball is held by one or more opponents, and one or more of his team-mates bind on to him. All the players involved are on their feet and moving towards a goal line. Players joining a maul must have their heads and shoulders no lower than their hips and endeavour to stay on their feet. The ball-carrier in a maul may go to ground providing play continues. Players must not intentionally collapse a maul, jump on top of it or attempt to drag an opponent out of it. Further, no player may take any action to make the opposing team think that the ball is out of the maul while it is still in it.

- If a player inside his own 22 makes a clean catch direct from an opponent's kick and at the same time shouts 'Mark!', he wins a free kick from that spot, which he himself should take. A mark cannot be made from a kickoff.

- If a mark is made in-goal, a scrum is awarded 5 m from the goal line. The team of the player who made the mark throws the ball in.

- The ball is in touch when either it or any player carrying it goes over or comes into contact with the touchline.

RUGBY UNION PLAYERS' NUMBERS AND POSITIONS

1	prop forward
2	hooker
3	prop forward
4	lock forward
5	lock forward
6	flank forward
7	flank forward
8	No 8 forward
9	scrum half
10	stand-off half
11	left wing three-quarter back
12	left centre three-quarter back
13	right centre three-quarter back
14	right wing three-quarter back
15	fullback

- When the ball has gone out of play along the touchline, the game is re-started with a throw-in to a line-out of two rows of opposing players. Players not taking part in the line-out must be at least 10 m behind the participating players, or on their own goal line if that is nearer.

- At least two players from each team must form a line-out; the maximum number permitted is decided by the team throwing in the ball. The opposing team may have fewer players in the line-out but they must not have more.

- The front of the line-out must be at least 5 m from the touchline. The back of the line-out must be no more than 15 m from the touchline. The line-out players of both teams form two parallel lines 1 m apart at right angles to the touchline. The throw-in must be straight and must travel at least 5 m before it first touches the ground or touches or is touched by a player.

- A player may take a quick throw-in without waiting for a line-out to form.

- When one team puts the ball into touch, the throw-in is normally taken by the other side. The exception is when a team takes a penalty kick, and the ball is kicked into touch: the throw-in is then taken by a player of the team that took the penalty kick. This applies whether the ball was kicked directly or indirectly to touch.

- The scrum is used to re-start play after minor infringements or stoppages. Eight players from each team, bound together in three rows per team, close up with their opponents so that the heads of the front rows are interlocked. This creates a tunnel into which a scrum half throws in the ball so that the front-row players can compete for possession by hooking the ball with either foot.

- The middle player in each front row is the hooker. The players on either side of the hooker are the props. The left-side props are the loose-head props. The right-side props are the tight-head props. The two players in the second row who shove on the props and the hooker are the locks. The outside players who bind onto the second or third row are the flankers. The player in the third row who usually pushes on both locks is the No. 8.

- The scrum is usually formed where the infringement or stoppage happened, but never less than 5 m from the touchline or goal line.

- The ball is thrown into the scrum by the scrum half of the team that did not commit the infringement. The scrum ends when the ball comes out.

- Any player may take a penalty or free kick with any kind of kick: punt, drop kick or place kick. A goal cannot be scored from a free kick, but in the case of a penalty, the team may choose whether to kick for position or to go for goal.

- If a team is awarded a free kick inside its own 22, it may gain ground whether the ball is kicked directly the resulting throw-in will be from the point at which the ball went out of play. However, if the free kick is awarded outside the kicker's 22 there is no gain in ground – the resulting throw-in is taken from a point in touch in line with the place where the kick was taken –

unless the ball bounces in play before going indirectly into touch, in which case the throw-in is taken from the spot where the ball went out of play.

GOVERNING BODY

International Rugby Football Board
Huguenot House
35/38 St Stephen's Green
Dublin 2
Ireland

Website: http://www.irfb.com

Showjumping

Showjumping tests the rider's skill and the horse's ability over a series of fences. The object is to ride 'a clear round'; in other words, to negotiate the whole course without knocking down any of the obstacles, dismounting, falling off or refusing to jump.

CLOTHING AND EQUIPMENT

- Military or hunt uniform (red or black coat, white shirt and tie, white breeches, hunting cap and black boots)
- Ladies may wear light fawn breeches and bowler hat or hunting cap

FIELD OF PLAY

The maximum length of a showjumping course is the number of obstacles multiplied by 60 m. The start and finish line and all fences are marked with a red flag on the right and a white flag on the left.

A typical grand prix showjumping course consists of 15 fences, each of a different type, as follows: a brush and rails; a double oxer, post and rails; double parallel poles; a double triple bar, planks and poles; a fancy gate; a hog's back; a narrow stile (two fences in one); oil drums with poles; poles over a bank; a post and rails; a stone wall; a treble vertical parallel; a water jump; a white gate.

Except in puissance, fences must not exceed 1.7 m in height or 2 m in spread (width to be jumped). Water jumps must not be greater than 4.5 m wide.

> ## PUISSANCE
>
> In this variant form of showjumping, there are four, five or six fences, each of which is at least 1.4 m high. In any puissance jump-off, the height and spread of fences may be increased, The name of this form of showjumping comes from the French meaning 'strength'.

RULES

- An obstacle is considered to be knocked down only when any part of it is knocked down or dislodged, even

if the falling part is arrested by another part of the obstacle. An obstacle may be touched, but there is no penalty unless all or part of it is dislodged. Displacements do not count against a rider if the fall occurs after he has crossed the finishing line.

- A rider may be penalised only once for each fence as a whole, no matter how many parts of it he may knock down during a jump.

- Any fall by horse or rider is penalised and the round must be re-started from the point at which it took place.

- A refusal occurs if a horse stops in front of an obstacle to be jumped. However, it is not a refusal if a horse stops in front of an obstacle and then jumps it from a standing position.

- A horse may be disqualified for disobedience if it is not fully under the control of the rider and avoids an obstacle it is supposed to have jumped, if it jumps an obstacle outside the boundary flags that surround the course, or if the rider fails to bring it back to jump the required obstacle.

- A horse may also be disqualified if it fails to pass the starting line within 60 seconds of the start of a round or if it takes more than 60 seconds to jump an obstacle, except following a fall.

- A disobedience or refusal is penalised by 3 faults the first time it occurs, the second time by 6 faults, and the third time by elimination. Faults for disobedience are cumulative, whether they occur at the same fence or not.

- Knocking down an obstacle or touching the water at a water jump counts 4 faults.

- There is a set time allowed for the completion of any course. Riders who take longer are penalised by ¼ of a fault per second or part of a second. The time limit is twice the time allowed.

- Faults are added together to give the competitor's score for the round or rounds.

- If, at the end of the competition, two or more entrants are equal on points, the winner is decided by a jump-off – further rounds of fences jumped by the tying competitors – until there is a winner.

GOVERNING BODY

Fédération Equestre Internationale
Ave Mon Repos 24
PO Box 157
1000 Lausanne 5
Switzerland

Website: http://www.horsesport.org

Skiing

Remnants of skis found in Sweden date from about 2500 BC. Modern skiing developed during the mid-19th century in Norway, where improvements made to bindings made it possible to jump and turn. Skiing has been an Olympic event since 1924; the first Alpine World Championships were held in 1931.

CLOTHING AND EQUIPMENT

- Warm waterproof clothing; tight-fitting to minimise wind resistance
- Goggles
- Skis: traditionally wooden, now usually synthetic material; no set dimensions
- Sticks (poles): steel or aluminium with a plastic handle and a disc known as a basket about 8 cm from the lower end to prevent loss in deep snow

---

FIELD OF PLAY

Courses (pistes) are marked with marker flags and gates, rectangular cloth panels at least 8 m wide hung between two poles. Some of them are put up to guide the skiers; others are used as control points for time-checks.

RULES

ALPINE SKIING

- There are three main types of competitive skiing: Alpine, Nordic, and the winter biathlon.

- In Alpine skiing, there are four events: downhill, slalom, giant slalom and Super-G (for Giant).

- Downhill is an all-out speed event; top-class competitors typically average more than 130 km/h. The piste is marked with only enough gates and directional flags to keep racers on the designated course and away from dangerous obstacles.

- Slalom is a test of turning ability in which the racer moves through a series of narrow, closely spaced gates at speeds of up to about 40 km/h. The slalom piste must be at least 40 m wide.

- In world and Olympic championships the overall vertical drop from top to bottom of the slalom course must be 180–220 m for men and 120–180 m for women. Slopes must have gradients of 33–45 per cent. Slalom poles are made of banners 75 cm wide and 50 cm high hung between two flexible stakes. Gates must be 4–6 m wide.

- Giant slalom and Super-G events involve elements of both downhill and slalom. Speeds average about 80 km/h (50 mph). The gates are farther apart than in

ordinary slalom. They are also wider – at least 4–8 m wide in giant slalom and at least 6–8 m in Super-G.

- The vertical drop in the giant slalom must be 250–400 m for men, and 250–350 m for women. In Super-G the drops are 500–650 m and 350–500 m respectively. The piste in both events must be no less than 30 m wide.

- In Super-G the maximum number of gates is the length of the vertical drop in metres divided by 10, with a minimum of 35 gates for men and 30 for women. The distance between the turning poles of successive gates must be 25 m

- In all Alpine events, competitors are divided into groups of 15. The starting order in the first round is determined by drawing lots or a similar method. In subsequent rounds the skiers start in order of the number of points they have previously scored. In both slalom and Super-G, competitors start at 60-second intervals.

NORDIC SKIING

- Nordic skiing consists of cross-country travel over undulating terrain. The standard distances for men are 10 km, 15 km, 30 km and 50 km in the individual events and a 4 x 10 km relay; women ski 5 km, 10 km and 20 km distances, and a 4 x 5 km relay.

- The Nordic ski course should ideally be divided into three sections: one-third undulating, one-third uphill, one-third downhill. The downhill section should not be at the end of the course.

- The maximum total climbs should be as follows: 150–225 m in 5 km races; 250–450 m in 10 km races; 400–650 m in 15 km races; 800–1,200 m in 30km races; and 1,400–1,800 m in 50 km races.

> The winter biathlon is a direct descendant of World War II military ski patrols. The sport made its Olympic début at Squaw Valley, California, USA in 1960.

- There are also two Nordic jumping competitions (for men), one on hills known as normal hills, with an average jump distance of over 70 m, and the other on large hills, with an average distance of over 90 m.

WINTER BIATHLON

- The winter biathlon combines cross-country skiing and shooting from both the standing and prone positions, with time penalties for missing targets along the course.

- There are four types of winter biathlon competition: individual, over 20 km for men and 15 km for women; sprint, over 10 km for men and 7.5 km for women; relays of 4 x 7.5 km for men and 3 x 7.5 km for women; and team events over 20 km for men and 15 km for women.

- Every biathlon course has four shooting ranges, and there must be at least 3 km of skiing between each of them. On reaching a range, competitors should load their rifles (non-automatic weapons of up to 5.6 mm calibre; no magnifying optical sights) with five rounds and fire in their own time (on skis or off) at five circular targets set out in a line 50 m distant. The first and third shoots are fired from the prone position; the second and fourth are standing. The standing targets are 115 mm in diameter; the prone targets are the same size but have a white bull's-eye measuring 45 mm in diameter.

- For each failure to hit the target, 2 minutes are added to the contestant's time, and for each shot in the outer ring, 1 minute is added.

- Rules for the relay and team biathlons may differ slightly from those above. The first skiers in the relay teams start at the same time, and the first firing range is at 2.5 km. Each competitor has eight rounds of ammunition for five targets. If he hits all the targets with the first five rounds he may continue to ski; if not, he must continue firing until he has either hit all the targets or let off all his rounds. If he still fails to hit five targets he must complete a 150 m handicap circuit for each missed target.

- The second firing range in the relay is at 5 km.

- At the handover, each skier sends the next man on his way with a pat on the back.

- In team biathlons, the teams start at 2-minute intervals and each team's skiers must race in serried formation (closed ranks) throughout, including across the finishing line. At each target area, one skier shoots while the rest of the team race to a waiting area in front of the handicap loop. If the shooter hits all five targets the team may continue. If he does not, they must do one lap of a 300 m handicap loop for every target missed.

GOVERNING BODY

Fédération Internationale de Ski
Worbstrasse 210
CH-3073 Gümligen bei Bern
Switzerland

Website: http://www.fis-ski.com

Snooker

Snooker originated in India in the late 18th century. In the 1980s, the game went from being a minority interest to the most popular sport on British television.

CLOTHING AND EQUIPMENT

- Professionals: black shoes, black trousers, a waistcoat and bow tie, white shirt
- Cues: wooden, no less than 3 ft long
- 22 balls: 2¹⁄₁₆ in in diameter of 15 reds, six colours (yellow, green, brown, blue, pink, black), and one white cue ball

FIELD OF PLAY

Snooker is played on a baize-covered table 34 in high measuring 12 ft by 6 ft with a playing area of 11 ft 8½ in x 5 ft 10 in. There are six pockets or holes (*see* diagram).

RULES

- The aim of the game in snooker is to score more points than the opponent.
- Play begins with the balls placed as in the diagram. The apex ball of the triangle of reds is racked as close as possible to the pink without touching it.

*Rests of various sorts can be used by the player to gain
access to the cue ball in difficult situations*

- Point values are red 1, yellow 2, green 3, brown 4, blue
  5, pink 6, black 7.

- The straight line drawn 29 in from the face of the
  bottom cushion and parallel to it is known as the baulk
  line and the intervening space is called baulk.

- The half-circle is a semicircle described in baulk with its
  centre at the middle of the baulk line and with a radius
  of 11½ in. When the striker has the cue ball in hand, he
  may place it anywhere on the line or within the half-
  circle, and may use his hand or any part of his cue

(including the tip) to position the cue ball, as long as he is not attempting to play a stroke.

LAGGING OR STRINGING

The first break is sometimes decided by a contest to see which player can get the cue ball closer to the top cushion by playing it from behind the baulk line, off the bottom cushion and back up the table.

- Players are awarded points for fouls by the opponent and for legally potting reds or colours. Each legally potted red and colour has the point value indicated above. A frame normally ends when all the balls have been potted apart from the cue ball. However, if either player may still win when only the black remains on the table, the frame ends with the first score or foul. If the players' scores are equal after the black has been potted, the ball is re-spotted on its original position and the players lag or string (*see* box) or toss for the choice of playing at, or assigning the opponent to play at, the black ball with the cue ball in hand within the half-circle. The first score or foul ends the frame.

- Players lag, toss or draw lots for choice of break in the opening frame, then break alternately in subsequent frames. The number of frames in a match is agreed before the start.

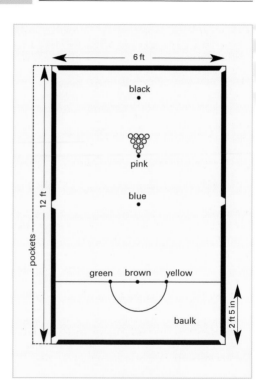

- The player who starts has the cue ball in hand within the half-circle. He must cause the cue ball to contact a red ball and failure to do so is a foul. When a foul is scored, the appropriate number of points is added to the score of the incoming player, who then has a choice of accepting the table and becoming the striker, or requiring the offender to break again.

- A legally potted ball entitles the striker to continue at the table until he fails to pot a ball legally. Failure to contact a legal object ball first is a foul.

- Any red balls potted on a legal shot are legally potted balls. If more than one red ball is potted in a single shot, each will score 1 point.

- When the striker has a red ball as his 'ball on' (legal object ball), he must cause the cue ball's first contact to be with a red ball. Failure to do so is a foul.

- After the striker has potted a red ball, his next legal object is a colour, and as long as reds remain on the table he must alternate his play between reds and colours (though within each group he may play any ball of his choice). When reds remain on the table and a colour is his object, the striker must (a) say before stroking which colour ball is his object and (b) cause the cue ball's first contact with a ball to be with that coloured ball. If the striker fails to meet these requirements, it is a foul.

- If the striker's ball on is a red and he pots a colour, it is a foul. If the striker's ball is on a colour and he pots any other ball, it is a foul.

- Jumping the ball and knocking it off the table are different fouls and should both be noted.

- While reds remain on the table, each potted colour is replaced on its spot before the next stroke. After a colour has been spotted, if the striker plays while that ball is incorrectly spotted (and opponent or referee calls it before two such plays have been taken), the shot taken is a foul. If the striker plays two strokes after such error without it being noticed by opponent or referee, he is free of penalty and play continues as if the error had not occurred.

- When no reds remain on the table, the striker then has to pot the colours in ascending order of value: yellow, green, brown, blue, pink, black. These legally potted colours are not re-spotted after each is potted; they remain off the table.

- Reds that are potted illegally or jumped off the table are not re-spotted; they remain off the table. Colours illegally potted or jumped off the table are re-spotted. In all cases, the striker has committed a foul.

- Reds are never spotted. Colours to be spotted are placed as at the start of the game. If a colour's spot is occupied,

and spotting it would make it touch a ball, it is placed on
the spot of the highest value colour that is unoccupied. If
all the spots are occupied, the colour is spotted as close
as possible to its original spot on a straight line between
its spot and the nearest point on the top cushion (i.e., the
end opposite baulk).

- If the cue ball is jumped off the table, it is a foul, and the
  incoming player begins his turn by placing the cue ball
  within the half-circle.

- While balls are in play it is a foul if the striker touches
  any object ball or if the striker touches the cue ball with
  anything other than the tip of his cue during a legal
  stroke.

- The cue ball is said to be snookered when a direct stroke
  in a straight line to any part of every ball on is obstructed
  by a ball or balls not on.

- If the cue ball is touching another ball which is, or
  can be, on, the referee or player shall state 'Touching
  ball'. Thereafter the striker must play away from it or
  it is a push stroke (foul). No penalty is incurred for
  playing away.

- A push stroke is a foul made when the tip of the cue
  remains in contact with the cue ball when the cue ball
  makes contact with the object ball, or after the cue ball
  has commenced its forward motion.

- The striker must try to hit the ball on. If the referee considers the rule infringed, he shall call 'A foul and a miss'. The incoming player may then play the balls as they lie, or request that the balls be returned to their original positions and have the offending player play the stroke again.

- After a foul, if the cue ball is snookered, the referee or player shall state 'Free ball'. If the non-offending player takes the next stroke, he may nominate any ball as on. For this stroke, the ball shall be regarded as, and acquire the value of, the ball on. If the free ball is potted, it is re-spotted, and the value of the ball on is scored. If the ball on is potted, it too is scored. If both the free ball and the ball on are potted, only the value of the ball on is scored.

- A player who commits a foul incurs the penalty prescribed (which is added to the opponent's score), and has to play again if requested by the next player. If more than one foul is committed in the same stroke the highest value penalty shall be incurred.

- Any foul on red, yellow, green or brown balls incurs a 4-point penalty. Fouls involving unlawful contact with or potting blue, pink or black incur penalties of 5, 6 and 7 points respectively.

- The following fouls also incur 4-point penalties, unless they are committed when the blue, pink or black are the balls on, in which case they cost 5, 6 and 7 points respectively: striking the cue ball when balls are still moving from the previous shot; hitting the cue ball more than once; playing without at least one foot on the floor; making the cue ball miss all object balls; sending the cue ball into a pocket; playing out of turn; laying a snooker with a free ball; playing a jump shot; pocketing a ball that is not on; playing a push stroke; touching a ball with anything other than the tip of the cue; forcing a ball off the table.

- If the cue ball simultaneously hits both the ball that is on and another ball, the foul awarded will be to the value of the higher-scoring ball.

- A 7-point penalty is also incurred in the following circumstances: if, after potting a red, the striker commits a foul before nominating a colour; if he uses a ball off the table for any purpose; if he plays at reds in successive strokes; or if he uses as the cue ball any ball other than the white.

GOVERNING BODY

World Professional Billiards and Snooker Association (WPBSA)

27 Oakfield Road
Clifton
Bristol BS8 2AT

Squash

Squash – or squash rackets, to give it its full name – was first played in the early part of the 19th century by pupils at the English public school Harrow. From here it has spread across the world.

CLOTHING AND EQUIPMENT

- Lightweight shirts and shorts or skirts, any colour
- Shoes with special heels and grips that do not leave marks on the court
- Racket: graphite with two layers of strings woven into a uniform pattern; strings may be gut, nylon or plastic; maximum weight 255 g
- Ball: diameter 39.5–40.5 mm; weight 23–24 g; several varieties, each play at different speeds; the slowest, used for top-class matches, is distinguished by a yellow dot, and the quickest, used by beginners, has a blue dot

FIELD OF PLAY

An indoor court measuring 9.75 m by 6.4 m (*see* diagram).

RULES

- A squash match is the best of three or five games. The winner of each game is the first player to score 9 points, except when the score reaches 8–all for the first time. At this point, the receiver may choose to continue that game either to 9 points (known as 'Set One') or to 10 points (known as 'Set Two'). In the latter case, both players need 2 clear points to win the game.

More than any other sport, squash has been dominated by a single family: the Khans from the village of Nawakille near Peshawar, Pakistan. The dynasty has so far won the world championship 30 times through Hashim Khan (1951–56, 1958), Roshan Khan (1957), Azam Khan (1959–62), Mohibullah Khan (1963), Jahangir Khan (1982–92) and Jansher Khan (1993–97).

- The player who will serve first is determined by the spin of a racket. The strings of every racket have a rough and a smooth side, and the caller predicts which side will face up when the racket falls after spinning.

- At the beginning of each game the server has the choice of serving from either box and thereafter shall serve from alternate boxes while remaining the server. However, if a rally ends in a let, the server shall serve again from the same box.

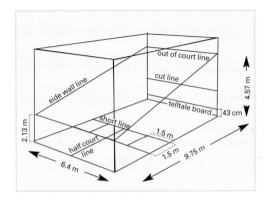

- At the start of any point, the server puts the ball in play while having one foot in the service box. To serve, you drop or throw the ball from either a hand or the racket before striking it. The ball must then hit above the service line on the front wall and rebound so that it hits the floor beyond the service-court line in the opposite half of the court.

- Points can be scored only by the server. If the receiver wins a stroke, he becomes the server. The server scores points until the service is lost. Service is lost when the server fails to hit the ball before it bounces twice, when the ball hits the 'telltale' – a metal strip 43 cm high at the bottom of the front wall – or when the server sends the ball above the out of court line.

- At the start of the second and each subsequent game, the winner of the previous game serves first.

- After a good service has been delivered, the players return the ball alternately until one fails to make a good return or there is an appeal by either player.

- If the ball, before reaching the front wall, hits the striker's opponent (including anything worn or carried), the striker wins the stroke if the return would have been good and the ball would have struck the front wall without first touching any other wall.

- If the striker chooses not to continue the rally due to a reasonable fear of striking the opponent, then the striker may appeal for a let. A let should be allowed if the referee believes – or in the absence of a referee, the players agree – that a reasonable possibility of striking the opponent did exist, and that the striker would otherwise have been able to make a good return. However, if in the opinion of the referee a winning return has thus been prevented, the striker shall win the stroke (this is to prevent deliberate obstruction).

- The correct method of appeal, whether a let or a stroke is sought by the player, is with the words 'Let please'.

GOVERNING BODY

World Squash Federation
6 Havelock Road
Hastings
East Sussex TN34 1BP

Website: http://www.worldsquash.org

Swimming

After the athletics track events, swimming is the largest Olympic sport.

CLOTHING AND EQUIPMENT

- Costumes should be tasteful, discreet and under no circumstances transparent
- Goggles and hats: may be worn if desired but are not compulsory

FIELD OF PLAY

Pools may be of varying lengths, but most competitions and all Olympic swimming events are held in pools 50 m long and 21 m wide divided into eight lanes, each 2.5 m across. There are blocks at the start at the end of each lane, raising the competitors 75 cm above the surface of the water.

RULES

- There are four major styles in competitive swimming: freestyle, backstroke, breaststroke and butterfly.

- Freestyle is invariably the front crawl, because this is by far the fastest swimming stroke. The stroke is performed chest-down in the water and involves carrying one arm forward out of the water to nearly full extension, while the other arm is below the surface making a pulling movement that propels the body through the water. The flutter kick is used to add some forward thrust, but serves mainly as a stabilising motion. Swimmers breathe in while turning the head to one side or the other, then exhale gradually while their faces are underwater. The breathing is repeated at regular intervals in accord with the pace of the stroke.

- The backstroke is similar to the crawl but is performed on the back and without the crawl's breathing requirement. One arm is carried over the head out of the water to prepare for the next stroke, while the arm in the water completes the forward-pulling motion. The flutter kick is used, as in the crawl.

- In breaststroke, leg and arm movements are simultaneous. The hands are carried together forwards from under the chest to full extension, and are then swept back parallel to the body. A frog kick is used: the legs are drawn up, with knees bent and each leg turned outward; the legs are then thrust back parallel to the line of the body. Arms and legs must not move out of the lateral plane. When in competition, a swimmer may be disqualified for letting his strokes enter the vertical plane.

- The most physically demanding of all strokes, the butterfly is similar to, and derived from, the breaststroke. Arm and leg movements are simultaneous, although the arm recovery after each stroke is accomplished over, rather than under, the water. This arm movement, reminiscent of a butterfly's flight, gave the stroke its name. The legs are used in a dolphinlike kick in which they remain close together and are alternately bent and straightened out at the knee in a vertical plane.

- The four basic stroke categories may also be combined into medley races, in which each of the four basic strokes is used by the swimmer or a team in a certain sequence.

- In each event, the competitor with the fastest entry-time is assigned the middle lane or, in pools with an even number of lanes, the lane to the right of the centre. The

OLYMPIC SWIMMING EVENTS

(for men and women except where specified)

50 m freestyle	200 m butterfly
100 m freestyle	100 m backstroke
200 m freestyle	200 m backstroke
400 m freestyle	200 m individual medley
800 m freestyle (women)	400 m individual medley
1,500 m freestyle (men)	4 x 100 m freestyle
100 m breaststroke	medley
200 m breaststroke	4 x 200 m freestyle relay
100 m butterfly	4 x 100 m medley relay

rest of the entrants are placed alternately to left and right in descending order of speed. Thus if entry-times are a true reflection of form, the swimmers will fan out into a spearhead formation as the race progresses.

- All races except backstroke events begin when the referee calls 'Take your marks'. The swimmers then step up on to blocks at the end of their lanes.

- The swimmers then assume their starting positions, leaning forward ready to dive. When they are all quite still, the starting signal is sounded. This may be a shot, a klaxon, a whistle or the word 'Go'.

- Backstroke races begin with a push-off from the side of the pool.

- In most races the referee may allow two false starts, but if there is a third break before the signal, the offending swimmer will be disqualified. In the USA, however, a single false start will lead to disqualification.

- Swimmers may also be disqualified for failing to touch the end of the pool when making their turns.

GOVERNING BODY

Fédération Internationale de Natation Amateur (FINA)
Ave de l' Avant-Poste 4
1005 Lausanne
Switzerland

Website: http://www.fina.org

Table Tennis

Table tennis began to be played in the 1880s when a toy manufacturer marketed a game under the trade name Ping-Pong.

CLOTHING AND EQUIPMENT

- Short-sleeved shirts, shorts or skirts in any one or two colours, apart from white; opposing players should wear different colours from each other
- Flat-soled shoes
- Bat: any shape, size or weight; must have a flat blade of even thickness; 85 per cent natural wood and covered with pimpled rubber on one or both sides; pimples may face inwards or outwards
- Ball: white or yellow celluloid or plastic; diameter 38.2 mm; weight 2.5 g

FIELD OF PLAY

Table tennis is played on a rectangular table measuring 3.6 x 1.5 m. The playing surface must be 76 cm above the ground. Across the centre of the table a net 15.25 cm high is suspended above the playing surface.

RULES

- The aim of table tennis is to score more points than the opponent.

- Play begins when one player serves the ball by throwing it up at least 15 cm from the palm of his hand and striking it with his bat. The ball must bounce twice – once on each side of the net – before being returned by the other player.

If it touches the net but the service is otherwise good, a let is played.

THE EXPEDITE SYSTEM

If, after 15 minutes' play, neither player has scored 19 points, each player serves a point in turn until the end of the match. If a receiver makes 13 good returns, he scores a point.

- All serves must be made diagonally, from the right-hand court into the opponent's right-hand court.

- The server serves for 5 points; the opponent then serves the next five, and so on. Players swap ends after each game.

- In doubles, players take it in turns to strike the ball. No player on either side may make two consecutive returns.

- The player or doubles team who first scores 21 points wins. However, you must win by 2 points, so a game could go on indefinitely. A match is usually the best of three games, but in international championships the best of five. At 20–20 and after, each player serves alternately.

- It is legal to hit the ball around the side of the net to land the ball on your opponent's side. Volleying (playing the ball before it has bounced) is not allowed.

- A player who touches the playing surface with his hand during a rally loses the point.

GOVERNING BODY

The International Table Tennis Federation
Ave Mon Repos 30
1005 Lausanne
Switzerland

Website: http://www.ittf.com

Target Shooting

Portable firearms were first used during the 14th century, but it was another five hundred years before guns were accurate enough for target shooting. Shooting has been an Olympic event since 1896.

CLOTHING AND EQUIPMENT

- Any clothing as long as it does not provide artificial support in the firing positions
- Guns: rifles, pistols and shotguns

FIELD OF PLAY

Shooting ranges where competitors may fire simultaneously shoulder to shoulder. Spectators are seated behind the marksmen.

RULES

- Rifle-shooting competitions are conducted in three categories: small-bore (.22 calibre), with targets set 55 yd away in international events; big-bore (over .25 calibre), in which distances are standard at 330 yd in international competition; and air rifles.

- Further subdivisions are based on the shooting position: prone, kneeling and standing. International rules require a set number of shots from all three positions.

- Pistol shooting includes matches for .22 calibre weapons, centre-fire pistols (usually .38 calibre), .45 calibre service pistols and .45 calibre semiautomatic pistols. Targets are at distances of 50 ft, 20 yd, 25 yd, 50 yd and 55 yd.

- Shotgun events are trap-shooting and skeet. Twenty-five shots are taken at saucer-shaped ceramic targets called clay pigeons.

- In trap-shooting, targets are released from a trap house (a spring-loaded device launching clay pigeons) 16 yd in front of the shooters, who are in a semicircle at five adjacent stations. Five shots are taken from each station.

- For skeet-shooting, high- and low-flying targets are launched from trap houses at either end of a semicircle 120 ft 9 in across that has eight shooting stations. One target from each house is shot at from every station by each contestant. These are followed by simultaneous launches of targets from both houses requiring two rapid-fire shots from four of the stations. This makes a total of 24 shots. The twenty-fifth and final shot is either a repeat of the first miss or an optional extra shot.

GOVERNING BODY

International Shooting Sport Federation
Bavariaring 21
D–80336 Munich
Germany

Website: http://www.issf-shooting.org

Tennis

Now the most popular racket game in the world, tennis – or lawn tennis, as it is strictly known, to distinguish it from real (royal) tennis – was patented in Wales in 1874 by Major Walter Wingfield under the name 'Sphairistiké'.

CLOTHING AND EQUIPMENT

- Rubber-soled shoes, socks, shorts or skirts and shirts, any colour, although Wimbledon still insists that overall look be predominantly white
- Balls: yellow or white with stitchless seams; diameter 2½–2⅝ in; weight approx. 2 oz; should bounce 53–58 in when dropped from 100 in onto flat, rigid surface
- Racket: maximum frame length 29 in; width 12½ in; maximum hitting surface 15½ in long, 11½ in wide; must be identical on both faces

FIELD OF PLAY

Tennis is played on a court with a grass, clay, tarmac or concrete surface measuring 78 ft long and 27 ft wide for singles, 36 ft wide for doubles. The net is made of cord mesh suspended from a metal cable that extends right across the middle of the court and 3 ft beyond the sidelines. The top of the net must be 3 ft above the ground and be held taut by posts at both ends and a vertical white strip at the centre.

RULES

- The aim of the game is to win two out of three or three out of five sets.

- Players stand on opposite sides of the net; the player who delivers the ball is the server, the other is the receiver. The receiver may stand where he pleases on his own side of the net. In doubles, the two players who are neither serving nor receiving service may also stand wherever they wish.

- Choice of ends and the right to serve or receive first are decided by toss. The player winning the toss may choose or require his opponent to choose either (a) whether to serve or receive first, or (b) which end to serve from or receive at first.

- The server must stand still with both feet behind the baseline, and within the imaginary continuations of the centre mark and sideline. The server tosses the ball into the air and strikes it with his racket before the ball hits the ground. Players may serve underhand or overhand.

- Each service is delivered alternately from the right and left halves of the court, beginning from the right in every game.

- The ball served should pass over the net and hit the ground within the service court which is diagonally opposite before the receiver returns it. If it doesn't, a fault is called.

- A player commits a foot fault if, while serving, either foot touches the court (including the baseline), any part of the imaginary extension of the centre mark, or any point beyond the imaginary extension of the outside edge of the sideline.

- After a fault (if it is the first fault) the server serves again from behind the same half of the court from which he served the fault. If he then serves another fault, he loses the point.

- A let is an agreement to play a point again, usually because of an interruption, as for example if the ball bursts. When a let is called in open play, the whole point is replayed; when it is called in respect of a service, that one service only is replayed.

- The service is a let if the ball served touches the net on its way into the opposite service court. A let is also called if a service is delivered when the receiver is not ready.

- If a player wins his first point, the score is called 15 for that player; on winning his second point, the score is called 30 for that player; on winning his third point, the score is called 40 for that player. If the player then wins a fourth point, he wins the game, unless his opponent has also won 3 points, in which case the score is deuce. After deuce, the game cannot be won until one player has 2 clear points; the next point won by either player at deuce is called advantage to that player. If the player at advantage loses the next point, the score returns to deuce.

> A player who has scored no points in a game or no games in a set is said to have 'love'. This is a corruption of the French word *oeuf*, meaning 'egg', which describes the shape of a zero.

- At the end of the first game in singles, the receiver becomes server, and the server the receiver, and so on alternately in all subsequent games.

- Players change ends after every odd-numbered game. The balls are changed after every seven games. A player with new balls should draw the opponent's attention to them by holding them up before he serves.

- The player who first wins six games wins a set, except that he must win by a margin of two games over his opponent. Where necessary, a set is extended until this margin is achieved.

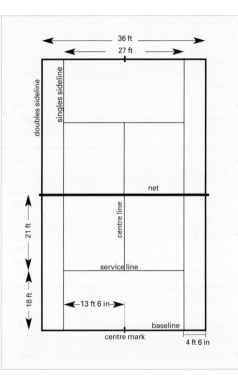

- As an alternative to carrying on a set until a two-game lead has been achieved, a tie-break may be played. The player who first wins 7 points wins the game and the set provided he leads by a margin of 2 points. If the score reaches 6–6 (6 points all), the game is extended until this margin is achieved.

- The player whose turn it is to serve is the server for the first point. His opponent is the server for the second and third points and thereafter each player serves alternately for two consecutive points.

- Players change ends after every 6 points and at the end of the tie-break.

- The player (or pair in the case of doubles) whose turn it was to serve first in the tie-break receives service in the first game of the following set.

- In doubles, the order of serving and receiving is decided at the beginning of each set. The pair who serve in the first game of each set decide which partner shall do so as and the opposing pair decide similarly for the second game. The partner of the player who served in the first game serves in the third; the partner of the player who served in the second game serves in the fourth, and so on in the same order in all subsequent games of the set.

- The pair who receive service in the first game decide

which partner receives the first service, and that partner
continues to receive the first service in every game
throughout that set. Partners receive service alternately
throughout each game.

- The server wins the point if the ball is served and then
touches the receiver or anything he wears or carries,
before it hits the ground.

- A player loses the point if he hits the ball into the net or
fails to return it over the net into the opponent's half of
the court before it has bounced twice. He also loses the
point if he deliberately hits the ball more than once.
Nevertheless, two hits occurring in the course of a single,
continuous swing do not constitute a double hit. Finally,
the point is lost if either the player or his racket touches
the net during play, or if he throws his racket at and hits
the ball, even if the ball then lands in the opponent's
court.

- A return is good if: the ball touches the net, provided
that it then hits the ground within the court; the ball hits
the ground within the proper court and rebounds or is
blown back over the net, and the player whose turn it is
to strike reaches over the net and plays the ball, provided
that he does not touch the net; the ball is returned
outside the posts, provided that it hits the ground within
the proper court; or a player's racket passes over the net

after he has returned the ball, provided that the ball
passes the net before being played.

• A ball falling on the line is in.

GOVERNING BODY

The International Tennis Federation (ITTF)
Bank Lane
Roehampton
London SW15 5X

Three-day Eventing

Three-day eventing is comprised of three distinct
equestrian competitions. Day One is **Dressage**. Day Two is
endurance. Day Three is **Showjumping**.

CLOTHING AND EQUIPMENT

• Dressage and jumping events: hunting dress or
  military uniform
• Cross-country sections: black boots, white breeches,
  polo-neck sweater or shirt
• Horses: over 14.2 hands (1.4 m)

FIELD OF PLAY

The exact layout of the three-day eventing showjumping course may vary, but there are between 10 and 15 fences with a maximum height of 2 m. One jump must resemble a road crossing and there must be two fly fences, each with a spread of up to 3–3.5 m, depending on the competition. In addition, where possible, there should be a ditch or a water jump.

RULES

- The endurance is in four phases: (A) roads and tracks; (B) steeplechase; (C) roads and tracks (again); and (D) cross-country. There are normally an average of three obstacles per 1,000 m in Phase B and four per 1,000 m in Phase D. Riders may take the course at their own pace. Phases A and C are normally ridden at the trot or slow canter; B and D are at the gallop.

- Riders may walk beside their horses in phases A and C, as long as they are mounted when they cross the finishing post. In phases B and D, however, there are penalty zones in which they will lose points for dismounting.

- Each phase has a time allowed. For every second over it, competitors lose 1 penalty point in phases A and C, 0.8 of a penalty point in Phase B, and 0.4 of a penalty point in Phase D.

- Refusals at obstacles are penalised as follows: first refusal 20 points; second refusal 40 points; fall of horse and/or rider 60 points.

- Showjumping penalties are as follows: for a first disobedience, 10 points; for knocking down an obstacle or a foot in the water, 5 points; for a second disobedience anywhere (not just at a re-taken fence), 20 points; for a fall by horse and/or rider, 30 points. Jumping a fence in the wrong order or a third disobedience in the entire event is punished by elimination.

- Exceeding the time allowed to complete the course costs ¼ of a point per second or part of a second. A competitor who takes more than twice the time allowed is eliminated.

GOVERNING BODY

Fédération Equestre Internationale
Ave Mon Repos 24
PO Box 157
1000 Lausanne 5
Switzerland

Website: http://www.horsesport.org

Volleyball

Volleyball was invented in 1895 by
William G. Morgan in Holyoke,
Massachusetts, USA. The game he
named 'mintonette' was intended
as a less strenuous alternative to
Basketball for older people.

CLOTHING AND EQUIPMENT

- Shirts and shorts in uniform team colour or colours;
  shirts numbered on chest and back
- Lightweight flat-soled shoes or barefoot with
  referee's permission
- No headgear or jewellery
- Ball: leather or rubber; circumference 65–67 cm;
  weight 260–280 g; pressure 0.3–0.325 kg/cm^2.

FIELD OF PLAY

Volleyball is played indoors or outdoors on a rectangular court 18 m long and 9 m wide with a perimeter area of at least 3 m in width. Across the middle of the court is a net 9.5 m wide and 1 m high which is suspended between two poles so that the top of it stands at a height of 2.43 m for men and 2.24 m for women.

The court is divided by a centre line which runs beneath the net. Parallel to this line are two further lines at distances of 3 m. These are the attack lines, which divide each team's front zone from its back zone.

> Volleyball is one of the few games with a temperature rule; play cannot continue if the air is colder than 16 °C (61 °F) or warmer than 25 °C (77 °F).

RULES

• Volleyball is played between two teams of six players. Up to six substitutes are allowed. The object is to score points in the course of hitting a ball with the hands across a net and within the boundaries of the court so that the opposing team cannot return the ball.

• Matches are usually the best of five sets. A set is usually won by the first team to score 15 points unless scores tie at 14–14, in which case play continues until one team gains a 2-point advantage. If the score then reaches 16–16, the first team to reach 17 wins. The fifth set may

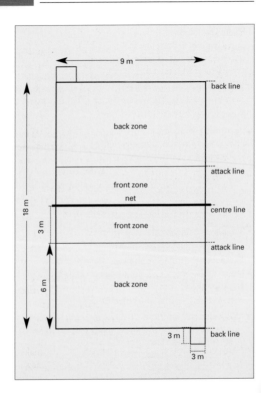

be decided by a tie-break using the rally-point system, in which either team may win a point, regardless of who served.

Beach volleyball is usually two-a-side. It began as a holiday recreation but is now an international and Olympic sport.

- The intervals between each set are 3 minutes long. Teams change ends after each set.

- At the start of every point, the team receiving service places three players – left, right and centre forwards – in the front zone and three in the back.

- The serving team has three forwards in the attack zone and two players in the back. The remaining player, the server, is positioned out of bounds in the service area beyond the backline on the right of the court.

- The server puts the ball into play with a one-handed strike, overarm or underarm, with an open palm. He may jump as he serves.

- Once the serve has passed over the net, the receiving team attempts to return the ball before it hits the surface of the court, using no more than three hits.

- If a serve goes out of bounds or fails to clear the net, play stops and the opposing team gains the serve.

- Front-row players may send the ball over the net (make an attack hit) at any height, but back-row players may do so only when they are in the back zone. If they play the ball in the front zone, they may make an attack hit only when at least half the ball is below the level of the net. Back-row players may not block the ball at the net.

- The ball may not be caught in the hands, and no player may hit the ball twice in succession during a single rally. If two or three players hit the ball simultaneously, this counts as two or three hits. Any part of the body may now be used to play the ball.

- Players may reach over into the opponents' side of the court while trying to play the ball, but they must not touch the net.

- At each change of service the players rotate one position clockwise so that each player has a chance to serve during the course of the game.

- Only when serving may a team score points: 1 point for each successful offensive rally. If the receiving team wins a rally, it gets to serve.

GOVERNING BODY

Fédération Internationale de Volleyball (FIVB)
Ave de la Gare 12
1000 Lausanne 1
Switzerland

Website: http://www.fivb.org

Weightlifting

Before the 20th century, weightlifting was primarily a stage- and circus feat. It became an Olympic sport in 1920.

Competitors attempt to raise above their heads a bar loaded with weights at each end.

Weightlifters are grouped into categories according to their weight.

CLOTHING AND EQUIPMENT

- One-piece leotard-like costumes, sometimes with T-shirts underneath and/or swimming trunks outside; belts may be no more than 120 mm wide
- Weights: the bar is 1.31 m long between the insides of the two barbells (the devices by which the weights are attached to the bar) and weighs 25 kg; barbells are 45 cm in diameter
- Additional weights are added in the form of discs which are colour-coded according to their weight: red 25 kg, blue 20 kg, yellow 15 kg, green 10 kg, white 5 kg, black 2.5 kg; in addition, there are three different chrome-coloured weights of 1.25 kg, 0.5 kg and 0.25 kg

FIELD OF PLAY

Weightlifting takes place on
a mat, usually indoors, often
on a raised platform

Powerlifting is a closely
related discipline which
sets more store by
sheer strength than
technique.

RULES

• In competition there are two different methods of lifting:
the snatch, and the clean and jerk. In the snatch, the lifter
grips the bar palms down and must pull it in a single
movement from the ground to the full extent of both
arms above his head. Finally, he must straighten his legs.

MEN		WOMEN	
Category	Maximum weight	Category	Maximum weight
1	52.0 kg	1	44.0 kg
2	56.0 kg	2	48.0 kg
3	60.0 kg	3	52.0 kg
4	67.5 kg	4	56.0 kg
5	75.0 kg	5	60.0 kg
6	82.5 kg	6	67.5 kg
7	90.0 kg	7	75.0 kg
8	100.01 kg	8	82.5 kg
9	110.0 kg	9	+82.51 kg
10	+110.01 kg		

- In the clean and jerk, the lifter grips the bar palms down, then brings it in a single movement to his shoulders while splitting or bending his legs. At this point he may rest the bar on his collarbones, chest or fully bent arms for as long as he likes until he is ready to raise the bar above his head. Once the bar is above the lifter's head, he must become motionless with his arms and legs extended and his feet on the same line. When the referee is satisfied that the lift has been properly completed, he will signal for the bar to be replaced on the ground. The bar must never be dropped.

- In both forms of competition the contestant's score is the combined weight of three lifts.

GOVERNING BODY

International Weightlifting Federation
H–1374 Budapest, Pf. 614
Hungary

Website: http://www.iwf.net

Windsurfing

Windsurfing began in Hawaii as a religious ceremony to appease the gods of the sea. It was almost eliminated in 1821 by European missionaries, who thought it immoral. In 1920, Duke Kahanamoku of Hawaii, an Olympic swimming champion, formed the first club in Waikiki and was largely responsible for popularising the sport.

CLOTHING AND EQUIPMENT

- Waterproof, one-piece, leotard-style knee- or ankle-length costumes
- Surfboards: lightweight balsa wood, fibreglass and polyurethane; any shape or size; typically weighing 11–18 kg; 1.8–3.7 m long; slightly rockered so that the middle is lower than the nose or tail, with a skeg, or fin, that acts as a lateral stabiliser
- Sail
- Mast

WINDSURFING COURSES

a   slalom course (1)
b   slalom course (2)
c   course racing

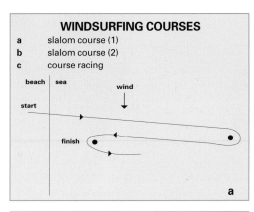

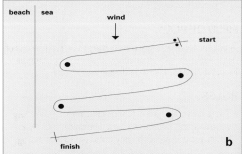

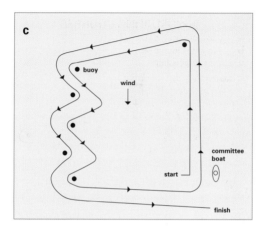

FIELD OF PLAY

Today the top places for windsurfing include the coasts of Australia, Brazil, England, New Zealand, Peru, Puerto Rico, South Africa, and California and Hawaii, USA.

RULES

• There are three basic categories in competitive surfing: course racing, slalom and wave performance. Other events include speed, freestyle and one-design racing.

- Course racing is held over a course marked out as in diagram c. Winds must be at least 11 knots. After 6-minute, 3-minute and 1-minute warnings comes the cry 'Go', on which all the racers start together, crossing an imaginary line about 100–200 m wide between the start boat and a buoy.

> The first commercial windsurfboard design was patented by Hoyle Schweitzer of California, USA in 1969.

- The winner scores 0.7 of a point; the surfer who comes second scores 2 points; third place gets 3 points and so on. At the end of a series (usually five or seven races), each competitor may discard his worst score and the winner is the surfer with the lowest points total.

- Slalom races are knockout contests held in heats of eight to ten racers at a time, with the first four or five contestants going forward to the next round. There are two main types of slalom course: the one that is chosen depends on the prevailing conditions. In large surf, there are usually only two buoys; in calmer conditions, there may up to six. The start is either from an imaginary line in the water as in course racing, or a Le Mans type, in which the surfers run from the beach and launch together. The wind minimum for professional slalom races is 12 knots.

- Wave performance races require a high degree of skill. They are 'man on man' (one against one in each race) knockout competitions, with the winner going forward to the next round. Heats usually last for 5 or 6 minutes.

- Points in wave performance windsurfing are scored in three categories: jumps, transitions and surfing. The more demanding and spectacular the moves, the higher the surfer's score will be. There is no maximum or minimum wave size, but the minimum wind is 12 knots.

GOVERNING BODY

International Surfing Association
5580 La Jolla Blvd, Suite 145
La Jolla
California 92037
USA

E-mail: surf@isasurf.org

Wrestling

Wrestling remains largely unaltered since the time of the ancient Egyptians. It was mentioned by Homer and featured in the 18th Olympic Games in 704 BC.

CLOTHING AND EQUIPMENT

- Tight-fitting, one-piece red or blue leotards
- Light knee-guards permitted
- Shoes must not have heels, nailed soles, rings or buckles
- Wrestlers must not cover their bodies with grease or oil; they must have short fingernails and be either cleanshaven or have full beards; stubble is not allowed

FIELD OF PLAY

Wrestling matches take place on a circular, padded mat with a diameter of 9 m. It may be raised to a level no higher than 1.1 m. In diagonal corners of the square which surrounds and encloses the ring are two triangular areas, one marked in red, the other in blue. These are the wrestlers' corners.

RULES

- In wrestling, two contestants attempt to pin each other's shoulders to the ground by employing different holds and body manoeuvres. There are two main codes, Freestyle and Greco-Roman, both of which feature in the modern Olympics.

• Freestyle wrestling is derived from early Greek wrestling, and the use of the legs is an integral part of these contests. The legs are used not only for balance and support but also for holding and lifting the opponent. Freestyle is the most popular wrestling form in the world and is used by both amateur and professional wrestlers.

- The Greco-Roman style permits no holds below the waist, and wrestlers are not allowed to use their legs for any grips.

- Before the start of a bout, the two wrestlers shake hands in the centre of the mat. After that they return to their respective corners, where they remain until the referee blows his whistle to start the match.

- One point is scored for bringing an opponent down in such a way that his whole back is on the mat; for moving from underneath an opponent to on top of him; and for applying a legitimate hold without causing the opponent to touch the mat with his head or shoulder.

- Two points are scored if an opponent is put into a rolling fall or if he rolls from side to side to form a bridge using his elbows and shoulders.

- Three points are scored for taking an opponent from the standing position to an immediate position of danger, that is, a position in which he bends beyond 90° with his back to the mat and resists with the upper part of his body.

- Five points are scored for a throw to an immediate position of danger.

- The following actions are forbidden: stepping on an opponent's feet; touching an opponent's face between eyebrows and mouth; gripping the throat; forcing an elbow or knee into an opponent's stomach or abdomen; gripping the edge of the mat; pulling an opponent's hair, flesh, ears, genitals or costume; twisting an opponent's fingers or toes; brawling, kicking, throttling and pushing; applying holds liable to endanger life, fracture limbs or torture into submission; bending an opponent's arm more than 90°; holding an opponent's head in both hands; scissor grips by the legs to an opponent's head or body; talking to an opponent; lifting an opponent from a bridge to throw him onto the mat.

> In the ancient Olympics, wrestlers were second only to discus throwers in popularity. Evidence that matches were increasingly being fixed and competitors bribed, however, brought the sport into disrepute and it was not revived until the 19th century.

- In addition, a wrestler applying a hold from behind in the standing position with his opponent's head down may throw the opponent to the side only and must ensure that part of his own body other than his feet touches the mat before his opponent's body.

- Greco-Roman wrestling also forbids seizing an opponent's legs, gripping an opponent with the legs and using the legs to push, lift or exert pressure when they are touching an opponent's body.

- Along with fouls, also forbidden are unsportsmanlike conduct, failing to obey the referee and passive obstruction, continually obstructing an opponent's holds, continually lying on the mat, wilfully running off the mat, or holding both an opponent's hands. Each infraction brings a caution; an opponent who receives three cautions in a bout is disqualified.

- A double head-hold (a double Nelson) is permitted as long as it is applied from the side and the legs are not used against the opponent's body.

WRESTLING WEIGHT DIVISIONS

Category	Maximum Weight
Light flyweight	48 kg
Flyweight	52 kg
Bantamweight	57 kg
Featherweight	62 kg
Lightweight	68 kg
Welterweight	74 kg
Middleweight	82 kg
Light heavyweight	90 kg
Heavyweight	100 kg
Heavyweight plus	130 kg

- Each bout lasts for 5 minutes without a break, unless one wrestler gains a 15-point lead, in which case the match is stopped (technical superiority). The timekeeper announces the time every minute. At the end of the bout, the timekeeper rings a bell and the referee then blows his whistle; no action is valid between bell and whistle.

- A fall is signalled by the referee striking the mat with his hand and blowing his whistle.

- If at the end of the bout there has been no fall and the two wrestlers are equal on points, sudden death overtime is played for an indefinite period until one wrestler scores a point.

GOVERNING BODY

British Amateur Wrestling Association
The Wrestling Academy
41 Great Clowes Street
Salford M7 1RQ

Website: http://www.sportsteacher.co.uk

CONVERSION TABLES

METRIC – IMPERIAL

KILOMETRES ► MILES		KILOMETRES ► YARDS	
km	mi	km	yd
1	0.621	1	1093.6
2	1.243	2	2187.2
3	1.864	3	3280.8
4	2.485	4	4374.4
5	3.107	5	5468.0
6	3.728	6	6561.6
7	4.350	7	7655.2
8	4.971	8	8748.8
9	5.592	9	9842.4
10	6.214	10	10 936.0
20	12.427	20	21 872.0
30	18.641	30	32 808.0
40	24.855	40	43 744.0
50	31.069	50	54 680.0
60	37.282	60	65 616.0
70	43.496	70	76 552.0
80	49.710	80	87 488.0
90	55.923	90	98 424.0
100	62.137	100	109 360.0

METRES ►	YARDS	METRES ►	FEET
m	yd	m	ft
1	1.094	1	3.281
2	2.187	2	6.562
3	3.281	3	9.843
4	4.374	4	13.123
5	5.468	5	16.404
6	6.562	6	19.685
7	7.655	7	22.966
8	8.749	8	26.247
9	9.843	9	29.528
10	10.936	10	32.808
20	21.872	20	65.617
30	32.808	30	98.425
40	43.745	40	131.234
50	54.681	50	164.042
60	65.617	60	196.850
70	76.553	70	229.659
80	87.489	80	262.467
90	98.425	90	295.276
100	109.361	100	328.084

CALCULATING AREA

m^2 ──────→ yd^2

In order to convert m^2 to yd^2, the formula below should be used:

$$m^2 \times 1.196 = yd^2$$

SQUARE METRES ▶	SQUARE YARDS
m^2	yd^2
1	1.196
2	2.392
3	3.588
4	4.784
5	5.980
6	7.176
7	8.372
8	9.568
9	10.764
10	11.960
20	23.920
30	35.880
40	47.840
50	59.800
60	71.759
70	83.719
80	95.679
90	107.639
100	119.599

CENTIMETRES ▶ INCHES		MILLIMETRES ▶ INCHES	
cm	in	mm	in
1	0.394	1	0.039
2	0.787	2	0.079
3	1.181	3	0.118
4	1.575	4	0.157
5	1.969	5	0.197
6	2.362	6	0.236
7	2.756	7	0.276
8	3.150	8	0.315
9	3.543	9	0.354
10	3.937	10	0.394
20	7.874	20	0.787
30	11.811	30	1.181
40	15.748	40	1.575
50	19.685	50	1.969
60	23.622	60	2.362
70	27.559	70	2.756
80	31.496	80	3.150
90	35.433	90	3.543
100	39.370	100	3.937

KILOMETRES PER HOUR	▶	MILES PER HOUR
km/h		mph
1		0.621
2		1.242
3		1.864
4		2.485
5		3.106
6		3.728
7		4.349
8		4.970
9		5.592
10		6.213
20		12.427
30		18.641
40		24.854
50		31.068
60		37.282
70		43.495
80		49.709
90		55.923
100		62.137

KILOGRAMS PER SQUARE CENTIMETRE	▶	POUNDS PER SQUARE INCH
kg/cm^2		PSI
0.6		8.534
0.8		11.378
1.0		14.223
1.2		17.068
1.4		19.912
1.6		22.757
1.8		25.601
2.0		28.446
2.2		31.291
2.4		34.135
2.6		36.980
2.8		39.824
3.0		42.669
3.2		45.514
3.5		49.781

KILOGRAMS ► POUNDS		GRAMS ► OUNCES	
kg	**lb**	**g**	**oz**
1	2.205	1	0.035
2	4.409	2	0.071
3	6.614	3	0.106
4	8.818	4	0.141
5	11.023	5	0.176
6	13.228	6	0.212
7	15.432	7	0.247
8	17.637	8	0.282
9	19.842	9	0.317
10	22.046	10	0.353
20	44.092	20	0.705
30	66.139	30	1.058
40	88.185	40	1.411
50	110.231	50	1.764
60	132.277	60	2.116
70	154.324	70	2.469
80	176.370	80	2.822
90	198.416	90	3.175
100	220.462	100	3.527

IMPERIAL–METRIC

MILES ▶ KILOMETRES		YARDS ▶ KILOMETRES	
mi	km	yd	km
1	1.609	100	0.091
2	3.219	200	0.183
3	4.828	300	0.274
4	6.437	400	0.366
5	8.047	500	0.457
6	9.656	600	0.549
7	11.265	700	0.640
8	12.875	800	0.731
9	14.484	900	0.823
10	16.093	1000	0.914
20	32.187	2000	1.829
30	48.280	3000	2.743
40	64.374	4000	3.658
50	80.467	5000	4.572
60	96.561	6000	5.486
70	112.654	7000	6.401
80	128.748	8000	7.315
90	144.841	9000	8.230
100	160.934	10 000	9.144

YARDS ► METRES		FEET ► METRES	
yd	m	ft	m
1	0.914	1	0.305
2	1.829	2	0.610
3	2.743	3	0.914
4	3.658	4	1.219
5	4.572	5	1.524
6	5.486	6	1.829
7	6.401	7	2.134
8	7.315	8	2.438
9	8.230	9	2.743
10	9.144	10	3.048
20	18.288	20	6.096
30	27.432	30	9.144
40	36.576	40	12.192
50	45.720	50	15.240
60	54.864	60	18.288
70	64.008	70	21.336
80	73.152	80	24.384
90	82.296	90	27.432
100	91.440	100	30.480

CALCULATING AREA

yd² m²

In order to convert yd² to m², the formula below should be used:

$$yd^2 \times 0.836 = m^2$$

SQUARE YARDS ▶	SQUARE METRES
yd²	m²
1	0.836
2	1.672
3	2.508
4	3.345
5	4.181
6	5.017
7	5.853
8	6.689
9	7.525
10	8.361
20	16.723
30	25.084
40	33.445
50	41.806
60	50.168
70	58.529
80	66.890
90	75.251
100	83.613

INCHES ▶ CENTIMETRES		INCHES ▶ MILLIMETRES	
in	cm	in	mm
1	2.54	1	25.4
2	5.08	2	50.8
3	7.62	3	76.2
4	10.16	4	101.6
5	12.70	5	127.0
6	15.24	6	152.4
7	17.78	7	177.8
8	20.32	8	203.2
9	22.86	9	228.6
10	25.40	10	254.0
20	50.80	20	508.0
30	76.20	30	762.0
40	101.60	40	1016.0
50	127.00	50	1270.0
60	152.40	60	1524.0
70	177.80	70	1778.0
80	203.20	80	2032.0
90	228.60	90	2286.0
100	254.00	100	2540.0

MILES PER HOUR	KILOMETRES PER HOUR	POUNDS PER SQUARE INCH	KILOGRAMS PER SQUARE CENTIMETRE
mph	km/h	PSI	kg cm^2
1	1.609	10	0.703
2	3.219	15	1.055
3	4.828	20	1.406
4	6.437	22	1.547
5	8.047	24	1.687
6	9.656	26	1.828
7	11.265	28	1.986
8	12.875	30	2.109
9	14.484	32	2.250
10	16.093	34	2.390
20	32.187	36	2.531
30	48.280	38	2.671
40	64.374	40	2.812
50	80.467	45	3.164
60	96.561	50	3.515
70	112.654		
80	128.748		
90	144.841		
100	160.934		

POUNDS ▶ KILOGRAMS		OUNCES ▶ GRAMS	
lb	kg	oz	g
1	0.454	1	28.349
2	0.907	2	56.699
3	1.361	3	85.048
4	1.814	4	113.398
5	2.268	5	141.747
6	2.722	6	170.097
7	3.175	7	198.446
8	3.629	8	226.796
9	4.082	9	255.145
10	4.536	10	283.495
20	9.072	20	566.990
30	13.608	30	850.485
40	18.144	40	1133.980
50	22.680	50	1417.475
60	27.216	60	1700.970
70	31.751	70	1984.465
80	36.287	80	2267.960
90	40.823	90	2551.455
100	45.359	100	2834.900

BIBLIOGRAPHY

American Football Ted Cox (Heinemann)

Bow and Arrow: The Comprehensive Guide to Equipment, Technique and Competition Larry Wise, Larry Wert (Stackpole Books)

Field Athletics (A & C Black)

Badminton John Edwards (Crowood Press)

Know the Game: Baseball and Softball (A & C Black)

Know the Game: Basketball (A & C Black)

Snooker and Billiards: Technique, Tactics, Training Clive Everton (Crowood Press)

How to Play Bowls M Shaw (Jarrold)

The Lonsdale Boxing Manual David James (Robson)

Canoeing Handbook Ray Rowe, Geoff Good (British Canoe Union)

Kayaking: A Beginner's Guide Nigel Foster (Fernhurst Books)

Wisden: The Laws of Cricket Don Oslear (Ebury Press)

Know the Game: Croquet (A & C Black)

Know the Game: Darts (A & C Black)

The Art of Swimming Steven Shaw, Armand D'Angour, Victoria Wood (Ashgrove Publishing)

An Illustrated Guide to Dressage Jennie Loriston-Clarke (Stephen Greene Press)

Fencing (Know the Sport) Allan Skipp (Stackpole Books)

Pocket Golf Rules Jonathan Vickers (HarperCollins Willow)

Gymnastics: A Guide for Parents and Athletes Rik Feeney
  (Masters Press)
Know the Game: Hockey (A & C Black)
Know the Game: Ice Skating (A & C Black)
Lacrosse Fundamentals Jim Hinkson (Warwick House)
Know the Game: Netball (A & C Black)
Riding: The Game of Polo Richard Hobson (J A Allen & Co Ltd)
Know the Game: Rounders (A & C Black)
Rowing and Sculling Bill Sayer (Robert Hale)
Know the Game: Rugby League (A & C Black)
Rugby Skills, Tactics and Rules Tony Williams, Gordon Hunter
  (Gill and Macmillan)
Showjumping for Fun or Glory Ernest Dillon, Helen Revington
  (Kenilworth Press)
The Complete Idiot's Guide to Skiing Claire Walter
  (Simon and Schuster)
Official Soccer Rules Illustrated Stanley Lover (Triumph Books)
Know the Game: Squash (A & C Black)
Know the Game: Table Tennis (A & C Black)
Airgun Field Target Shooting Les Herridge, Ian Law, Brian
  Hughes (Peter Andrew Publishing Co)
Know the Game: Tennis (A & C Black)
Know the Game: Volleyball (A & C Black)
The Weightlifting Encyclopedia Arthur Dreschler
  (A is A Communications)
The Ultimate Guide to Windsurfing Nik Baker, Daida Ruano
  Moreno (HarperCollins Willow)
This is Wrestling (Cadogan Guides)